Notting Hill Editions is an independent British publisher. The company was founded by Tom Kremer (1930–2017), champion of innovation and the man responsible for popularising the Rubik's Cube.

After a successful business career in toy invention Tom decided, at the age of eighty, to fulfil his passion for literature. In a fast-moving digital world Tom's aim was to revive the art of the essay, and to create exceptionally beautiful books that would be cherished.

Hailed as 'the shape of things to come', the family-run press brings to print the most surprising thinkers of past and present. In an era of information-overload, these collectible pocket-size books distil ideas that linger in the mind.

Louisa May Alcott (1832–1888) was an American writer best known as the author of the novel *Little Women* (1868) and its sequels *Little Men* (1871) and *Jo's Boys* (1886). Raised in New England by transcendentalist parents, Alcott grew up among many well-known intellectuals of the day, such as Ralph Waldo Emerson and Nathaniel Hawthorne. Having realised early in life that her father was too impractical to provide for his wife and four daughters and after the failure of Fruitlands, a utopian community that he had founded, Alcott's lifelong concern became the welfare of her family. To support them she taught briefly, worked as a domestic, and wrote, producing potboiler novels, at first, and many stories under pseudonyms. At the age of thirty, she volunteered as a nurse during the American Civil War but was sent home after contracting typhoid from unsanitary hospital conditions. The publication of her account of being a nurse, *Hospital Sketches* (1863), brought her her first taste of fame before the publication of *Little Women*.

Liz Rosenberg is the author of two biographies: *House of Dreams: A Biography of L. M. Montgomery* and *Sorrows, Scribbles and Russet Leather Boots: A Biography of Louisa May Alcott*. She is a Chancellor Award-winning professor of English at the State University of New York at Binghamton, and the author of numerous prize-winning books of fiction, poetry, and works for young readers.

Jane Smiley is the author of many novels and works of non-fiction. Her latest novel is *A Dangerous Business*, a mystery set in 1850s Monterey, California, and her latest non-fiction book is *The Questions that Matter Most*. She writes in many genres and she won the Pulitzer Prize in 1992 for *A Thousand Acres*.

A STRANGE LIFE

Selected Essays
of Louisa May Alcott

–

Edited and Introduced by
Liz Rosenberg

Preface by
Jane Smiley

nh Notting Hill Editions

Published in 2023
by Notting Hill Editions Ltd
Mirefoot, Burnside, Kendal LA8 9AB

Series design by FLOK Design, Berlin, Germany
Cover design by Tom Etherington
Creative Advisor: Dennis PAPHITIS

Typeset by CB Editions, London
Printed and bound by Memminger MedienCentrum,
Memmingen, Germany

A CIP record for this book is available from the British Library

ISBN 978-1-912559-43-5

nottinghilleditions.com

Contents

JANE SMILEY

– Preface –

W hen we were growing up, there were plenty of books we read on our own, and one of them, for me, was *Little Women* (1868). It was famous, it was for girls, and every library had lots of copies. It was easy to read, and the best part about it was that you could attach yourself to any of the four girls – Meg, the beauty, Jo, the independent one who likes writing, Beth, the sweetheart, or Amy, the youngest, who wants to be an artist. I was an only child, and I think, for me, reading *Little Women* was like observing one of our neighboring families in more detail than was possible by visiting or peeking through the window (even though I liked to try). The other book series I enjoyed, The Bobbsey Twins, Nancy Drew, and children's horse books, had no literary pretensions, so I think *Little Women* also showed me not only how to depict different personalities in a way that was complex and understandable, but also what it felt like to be alive in a historic period that I knew was important.

The sad and dramatic life that Alcott herself endured is well depicted in the introduction to this collection. I knew nothing about that when I was young, but now that I have been writing for many years, I can clearly see how Alcott's character and her experiences meshed when she began to write. She wanted to be independent, she wanted to explore, she wanted to help her family, because her father, Bronson, or Amos Bronson, was well-meaning but unable to provide for them most of the time (let's call him a prescient and intelligent vegetarian pre-hippie). He was also friends with American writers who lived in their neighborhood and who have now been immortalized by their own unique inventions: Henry David Thoreau, Ralph Waldo Emerson and Nathaniel Hawthorne. Because of these connections, Alcott would have understood that writing was a form of independent expression that challenges readers and also shows the author herself what she is really thinking and feeling. But because of the financial ups and downs of her family, whatever Alcott wanted to express in her work often had to be put aside so that she could write something that made money.

Alcott didn't want to write a girls' book – she thought that the essays and the books she was writing under her pen name, A. M. Barnard, were more interesting. But her editor prodded her and when she finally got started, she experienced something that I've also experienced – imagining the characters, setting and plot of your book carries you away, and after a bit, and maybe a rough start, the words and ideas seem to flow out of you and onto the page – who you are and what you know seeps into everything you write even when you aren't trying to make a statement. *Little Women* turned into a pleasure for Alcott, and sparked *Little Men* (1871) and *Jo's Boys* (1886). I can relate to that, too. Every writer knows that you can't predict which of your works is going to make money and which is going to fade into the background. You always retain a different attachment to each one, but as your career progresses, you learn more and more about how your readers feel by understanding which ones they prefer.

Alcott is so fascinating as a person and a writer that many biographies have been written about her (and several about her father). One of the dilemmas of being a novelist is how much of your own experiences, and of your own character, are you going to allow into your work? You are supposed to be writing fiction, and often your novels are inspired by things you have overheard, witnessed or read about. Something that struck you, even if it was a simple remark, made you curious to investigate whatever it was, and the novel you plan is not about you – in fact, there might be things in your mind or your past that you would like to keep to yourself – but you are who you are, and those things seep into the novel you are writing. I think that, for readers, one of the most fascinating things about *Little Women* is what Alcott may be divulging about her own life. I think I've read *Little Women* five times, most recently when I was asked to write an essay about one of the sisters. I chose Amy because I noticed things about her that I hadn't noticed before – that in a lot of ways her life prefigured the modern lives of girls (school, ambition, bullying, relationships, coming up on her own with a way to navigate the complexities of her existence while her parents are overwhelmed with other issues). Certainly, Jo, with her literary ambitions, resembles Alcott herself, and Amy resembles her artist sister May. But the danger of allowing your friends or family into your work is that characters have to behave like characters – with good qualities and bad ones, in order to make the plot interesting. The thing is, as hard as you try to keep them out of your work, because you are fond of them or loyal to them, they are what you know – and when I was writing my essay about Amy, I wondered if May ever read *Little Women* and was annoyed by the portrayal of Amy.

But maybe she was happy or amused to be included – a friend of mine appeared in my novel *Duplicate Keys*, as well as in the novels of The Last Hundred Years Trilogy, and a short story or two. Part of the reason was that sometimes I had to include a soldier who had actually seen war. A few years ago, he said to me, with a laugh: 'How many times are you going to kill me off?' I replied: 'You write what you know,' but I should have said: 'You write what you want to know.'

It seems to me that one of Alcott's principal characteristics was her curiosity, and 'Hospital Sketches', the essay in this volume about her experiences during the Civil War, reveals that – she knows it's dangerous, she knows that anything could happen, she knows she will see lots of things that are sad and maybe even traumatic, but she wants to help, and more than that, she wants to find out what there is to know. The way she writes about what she witnesses as a nurse is maybe the most idiosyncratic and interesting depiction of war that I have ever read – she is alert to the torments and also the absurdities of the day-to-day life of the hospital and how the patients and the nurses do their best to put up with them. She has a woman's perspective – she doesn't write about courage or strategy, victory or defeat, she writes about the peculiarities of survival. We know that her experience must have been traumatizing, but her fascination with details keeps her going.

Alcott's work, especially *Little Women*, is much loved, but it doesn't gain her the respect that we accord to Jane Austen, Virginia Woolf or George Eliot. I think that the essays in this book show that she was at least as interesting and original in her way of looking at her world as these three (all of whose novels I love) are. She offers a view of the nineteenth century that we haven't seen before, and that is extremely enlightening.

– Introduction –

L ouisa May Alcott is best known for her classic
American novel for young readers *Little Women*
(1868), but she earned her first taste of literary celebrity
as an essayist. That should surprise no one for her writing genius defied genre. In many ways, her finest essays
are even more brilliant – or perhaps more *consistently*
brilliant – than her novels and stories. Three of these
essays alone – 'Hospital Sketches' (1863), 'Transcendental Wild Oats' (1873) and 'How I Went Out to Service' (1874) – are, as they used to say in Charles II's day,
worth the price of admission. Anyone who has read
and loved any of her novels will recognize her charac-
teristic style, energy and wit in them.

Louisa May Alcott was born in 1832 into a family
of high idealists: lovers of equality, ideas and books.
Her first playthings, as a toddler, were her father's vol-
umes from his private library and she composed her
first poem, 'To the First Robin', when she was eight.
She learned to express herself and share her observations of the world in the childhood journals her
parents required their four daughters to keep and in
her early written observations, Alcott identifies and
scorns hypocrisy, especially when it harms the poor,

the helpless and the young. Later, in journals and letters written in her teens (precursors of her non-fiction), she exercises the eagle eye of a reporter; she is irreverent and astute. For instance, she described the highly-respected Julia Ward Howe, author of the American anthem 'Battle Hymn of the Republic', as a 'straw colored supercilious lady with pale eyes and a green gown in which she looked like a faded lettuce.' Her elders would have been appalled had they read her notes.

In line with the literary and social ideals of her family, Alcott's education was eccentric, yet exalted. As one of the founders of American Transcendentalism – that abstract American cousin to British Romantism – Alcott's eccentric philosopher father Bronson Alcott encouraged great figures like Ralph Waldo Emerson, Henry David Thoreau, Margaret Fuller and Nathaniel Hawthorne to educate his daughters. While Emerson loaned Alcott books from his library, Thoreau became her first earth science teacher, escorting the four Alcott sisters on nature walks and canoe rides, pointing out the flora and fauna (and more fancifully, the fairies) of New England.

Alcott's first published 'real' book, as she called it, was called *Flower Fables,* published in December, 1854. It was a collection of fairy tales written for Ellen Emerson, the daughter of Ralph Waldo Emerson. Inscribing the first copy to her mother, Alcott wrote: 'I hope to pass in time from flowers and fables to men and realities', which, of course, she did in both her essays and her novels for young people.

In one of the stand-out essays in this collection, 'How I Went Out to Service', Alcott records her labors as a young, naïve and over-worked domestic servant. When Alcott was about fifteen, her mother began an informal employment agency geared to help the poor and Alcott became one of her early 'clients', going out to keep house for a miserly lawyer in Dedham, Massachusetts.

The essay is as deft as anything she ever wrote. Alcott's sanctimonious minister-employer proves to be a liar, glutton and predator with designs on the poor young author. 'He presented me with an overblown rose, which fell to pieces before I got out of the room, pressed my hand, and dismissed me with a fervent "God bless you, child. Don't forget the dropped eggs for breakfast."' Part of the tragi-comedy in the essay is that throughout the innocent narrator doesn't see his misbehavior coming, but the reader does. Much like a narrator from a Jane Austen novel, Alcott sees, but does not understand, what lies ahead.

In 1861, the unknown Alcott presented this essay to Boston's most distinguished publisher, James Field, at the newly-created *Atlantic Monthly*. He glanced through the piece and dismissed her with a condescending: 'Stick to your teaching, Miss Alcott. You can't write.' To add insult to injury, he offered her forty dollars as a loan to start her own school. Luckily for us

all, a quiet young editor named Thomas Niles sat beside
Fields during this interview, listening in. Years later, he
would commission, edit and publish *Little Women*.

Alcott's first truly successful published essay was
'Hospital Sketches', based on her own experience of
being a nurse in the American Civil War. It captured
the attention of a reading public hungry for news of
the war, but it was not written with an eye toward
fame. Culled from letters home and journal notes,
Alcott herself thought it a hodge-podge of writing and
chronicles, unlikely to interest anyone: she was simply
recording her experiences and she was more shocked
than anyone when it became a popular sensation. First
published in serial form and later, in 1863, as a book,
'Hospital Sketches' provided rare on-the-ground re-
portage of the long, bloody conflict from a war nurse's
perspective – a thing unheard of at the time. It features
a narrator called 'Nurse Periwinkle', though nearly
everything else in it derives from real life. Alcott herself nursed sick and dying Union soldiers; witnessed
their arrival from the catastrophic battle at Fredericksburg and served as head of the night ward after only
two weeks on the job. 'It was a strange life: asleep half
the day, exploring Washington the other half, and all
night hovering, like a massive cherubim, in a red rigolette, over the slumbering sons of man.' She also con-
tracted typhoid pneumonia that nearly killed her, and
was heavily dosed with the wonder drug calomel, the
mercury poison that finally did.

Grateful nineteenth-century readers found, in 'Hospital Sketches', their first real-life account of the soldiers' experiences of the Civil War. Alcott's was new journalism before the phrase was ever invented, and readers embraced it. War news traveled northward slowly and unreliably, but 'Hospital Sketches' filled the gap for anxious Yankee families and friends. Still, Alcott was amazed by its reception: 'I cannot see why people like a few extracts from topsy-turvy letters written on inverted tea kettles,' she marveled. Only later did she admit that these autobiographical and realistic essays 'pointed the way' toward her true writing material and style.

Since some of the essays in this collection are very long, I have occasionally trimmed the text by using ellipses, taking care to keep flavor and meaning intact. They are also not presented here in chronological order. One of the latest is an autobiographical essay based on Alcott's unhappy early childhood experience on a communal farm. Written in 1873, 'Transcendental Wild Oats' alternates broad comedy with tragedy as it records in detail the near dissolution of the Alcott family. The commune, even at its most populous, was too small to succeed, and it housed eccentrics and bona fide lunatics equally. The utopian experiment was a dismal failure, for the commune and for the Alcotts personally, who nearly froze and nearly starved, and at the end of it all Bronson suffered a breakdown.

Surely these events were traumatic for a ten-year-old child, and this may partially explain why Alcott waited to write about it so late in life. But Alcott never lingers on the psychological devastation. Instead of dwelling in the self-reflection typical of memoir, she focuses on the characters around her and records the homely details of daily life ('unleavened bread, porridge, and water for breakfast; bread, vegetables, and water for dinner; bread, fruit, and water for supper'), leaving little room for disbelief. It must all be true, because it *sounds* true. Indeed that is part of her genius as an essayist and memoirist: she is as succinct as a newspaper reporter. Her prose canters along; she covers great distances in the fewest words; there is no dilly-dallying. Alcott once advised an aspiring writer: 'The strongest, simplest words are best.'

On more than one occasion she halted publication of her non-fiction work because she felt it was not true, not deep enough. This happened with a linked series of European travel essays, excerpted here from an unfinished collection of her travel writing called *Shawl Straps*. Another piece, intended as a travelogue of American places, she cut short early on, fearing that writing superficially might become a bad habit. She refused to become an imitation of herself.

Nor was she able or willing to keep a straight face throughout. In her lighter tone – for her tone, throughout her essays, is flexible – she captures, for example, the comic anxiety of the amateur traveler: 'put my tickets in every conceivable place . . . and finish by losing them entirely. Suffer agonies till a compassionate neighbor pokes them out of a crack with his pen-knife.'

Her essays are rich with unerasable moments, and as in her greatest works of fiction, they strike the intersecting point between tragedy and comedy. If she tugs on heartstrings in these essays – and most assuredly she does – she also demonstrates a clear awareness of the funny side of life.

Alcott understood that habitual use of humor and exaggeration might incline readers to doubt the veracity of her non-fiction and at the end of 'Hospital Sketches', she urges the reader to believe what is only partly true: 'such a being as Nurse Periwinkle does exist, that she really did go to Washington, and . . . these Sketches are not romance.' Her fiction found its roots in real-life experiences and her non-fiction always contained kernels of invention. Most of the time she shrugged off strict distinctions between fact and fiction.

Similarly, Alcott's essays always showcased her beliefs in abolition, suffrage and equal rights. (Although her language does not always accurately reflect this, for instance when she refers to 'colored people'.) Perhaps because her mother had labored in Boston's worst slums, campaigning tirelessly for healthier, safer working conditions, fair pay and equal opportunity, Alcott became a vocal supporter of the rights of women to vote, early and late, and shared her mother's dedication to such causes.

One of the essays here, 'Happy Women', fiercely defends women's inalienable right to remain single. In her fiction for young readers, she became known as 'The Children's Friend', an accolade that was both enriching (financially and otherwise) and limiting. Essay writing allowed her to say openly what her children's stories could only suggest.

After the enormous success of 'Hospital Sketches', her serious novels – *Moods* (1864) and *Work* (1873) – were published, but received tepid reviews at best and poor sales. Had these – or any of her subsequent gothic novels, published under a series of pseudonyms – succeeded, we might never have had *Little Women*, nor any of its sequels. As it was, Alcott tumbled into children's literature. In the 1860s and 70s a new pseudonymous 'Oliver Optic' series of books for boys flooded a new market and Thomas Niles, the young editorial assistant who had seen 'How I Went Out to Service' rejected out of hand, wanted to test the publishing waters for girls, believing there was a vacuum waiting to be filled. He used a blend of charm, encouragement and family pressure to persuade Alcott to try her hand at a girl's juvenile novel. Privately she noted in her journal: 'I plod away, though I don't enjoy this sort of thing. Never liked girls or knew many, except my sisters; but our queer plays and experiences may prove interesting, though I doubt it.' The one saving grace, she believed, was the story's reality: 'we lived it.'

Alcott's autobiographical essays, such as 'Hospital Sketches', 'Transcendental Wild Oats' and 'How I Went Out to Service', are closer in tone, style, voice and subject matter to *Little Women* than any of her early fiction, and if one wants to see the author of the March family chronicles in the making, one need look no further than into these essays. Even if they were not the literary jewels they are, they would be worthy of attention and it's not often that we get to see a great author coming into her own before our eyes.

As a woman and as an author, Alcott was a force of nature. For most of her life she wrote for eight hours a day, in addition to her other labors, which included scrubbing and sewing throughout the night, cleaning and cooking and teaching school. A side effect of the mercury poisoning she suffered as a result of the typhoid pneumonia meant that Alcott often wrote with an aching arm and a painfully swollen leg propped up on a stool. But throughout her life, the writing 'machine', as she called herself, had to keep producing in order to earn money to keep 'The Pathetic Family' (her private name for the Alcotts) afloat. She could not afford to sentimentalize or write lengthy and rambling descriptions; or to hold forth like her father. She knew she must please the public or starve.

None of these essays collected here were ever intended to be her 'real' work – that ambition she reserved for her unsuccessful literary adult novels – but the warm reception of 'Hospital Sketches' gave her confidence to trust her own voice and material. Without that 'hint', as she called it, she never could have written *Little Women* and it proved to her that readers crave truth as well as invention. Under the most challenging circumstances, she kept on writing, celebrating the good and calling out the bad. She rejected sentimentality and self-pity in an era that encouraged both, especially for women who were expected to faint away at the first obstacle. That was not Louisa's way. 'I was there to work, not to wonder or weep . . .'

– How I Went Out to Service –
(1874)

When I was eighteen I wanted something to do. I had tried teaching for two years, and hated it; I had tried sewing, and could not earn my bread in that way, at the cost of health; I tried story writing and got five dollars for stories which now bring a hundred; I had thought seriously of going upon the stage, but certain highly respectable relatives were so shocked at the mere idea that I relinquished my dramatic aspirations.

'What *shall* I do?' was still the question that perplexed me. I was ready to work, eager to be independent, and too proud to endure patronage. But the right task seemed hard to find, and my bottled energies were fermenting in a way that threatened an explosion before long.

My honored mother was a city missionary that winter, and not only served the clamorous poor, but often found it in her power to help decayed gentlefolk by quietly placing them where they could earn their bread without the entire sacrifice of taste and talent which makes poverty so hard for such to bear. Knowing her tact and skill, people often came to her for companions, housekeepers, and that class of the needy who do not make their wants known through an intelligence office.

One day, as I sat dreaming splendid dreams, while I made a series of little petticoats out of the odds and ends sent in for the poor, a tall, ministerial gentleman appeared, in search of a companion for his sister. He possessed an impressive nose, a fine flow of language, and a pair of large hands, encased in black kid gloves. With much waving of these somber members, Mr R set forth the delights awaiting the happy soul who should secure this home. He described it as a sort of heaven on earth. 'There are books, pictures, flowers, a piano, and the best of society,' he said. 'This person will be one of the family in all respects, and only required to help about the lighter work, which my sister has done herself hitherto, but is now a martyr to neuralgia and needs a gentle hand to assist her.'

My mother, who never lost her faith in human nature, spite of many impostures, believed every word, and quite beamed with benevolent interest as she listened and tried to recall some needy young woman to whom this charming home would be a blessing. I also innocently thought: 'That sounds inviting. I like housework and can do it well. I should have time to enjoy the books and things I love, and D is not far away from home. Suppose I try it.'

So, when my mother turned to me, asking if I could suggest anyone, I became as red as a poppy and said abruptly: 'Only myself.'

2

'Do you really mean it?' cried my astonished parent.

'I really do if Mr R thinks I should suit,' was my steady reply, as I partially obscured my crimson countenance behind a little flannel skirt, still redder.

The Reverend Josephus gazed upon me with the benign regard which a bachelor of five and thirty may accord a bashful damsel of eighteen. A smile dawned upon his countenance, 'sicklied o'er with the pale cast of thought', or dyspepsia; and he softly folded the black gloves, as if about to bestow a blessing, as he replied, with emphasis:

'I am sure you would, and we should think ourselves most fortunate if we could secure your society, and – ahem – services for my poor sister.'

'Then I'll try it,' responded the impetuous maid.

'We will talk it over a little first, and let you know tomorrow, sir,' put in my prudent parent, adding, as Mr R arose: 'What wages do you pay?'

'My dear madam, in a case like this let us not use such words as those. Anything you may think proper we shall gladly give. The labor is very light, for there are but three of us and our habits are of the simplest sort. I am a frail reed and may break at any moment; so is my sister, and my aged father cannot long remain; therefore, money is little to us, and anyone who comes to lend her youth and strength to our feeble household will not be forgotten in the end, I assure you.' And, with another pensive smile, a farewell wave of the impressive gloves, the Reverend Josephus bowed like a well-sweep and departed.

'My dear, are you in earnest?' asked my mother.

'Of course, I am. Why not try this experiment? It can but fail, like all the others.'

'I have no objection; only I fancied you were rather too proud for this sort of thing.'

'I am too proud to be idle and dependent, ma'am. I'll scrub floors and take in washing first. I do house-work at home for love; why not do it abroad for money? I like it better than teaching. It is healthier than sewing and surer than writing. So why not try it?'

'It is going out to service, you know, though you are called a companion. How does that suit?'

'I don't care. Every sort of work that is paid for is service; and I don't mind being a companion, if I can do it well. I may find it is my mission to take care of neuralgic old ladies and lackadaisical clergymen. It does not sound exciting, but it's better than nothing,' I answered, with a sigh; for it *was* rather a sudden down-fall to give up being a Siddons and become a Betcinder.

How my sisters laughed when they heard the new plan! But they soon resigned themselves, sure of fun, for Lu's adventures were the standing joke of the family. Of course, the highly respectable relatives held up their hands in holy horror at the idea of one of the clan degrading herself by going out to service. Teaching a private school was the proper thing for an indigent gentlewoman. Sewing even, if done in the seclusion of home and not mentioned in public, could be tolerated. Story-writing was a genteel accomplishment and reflected credit upon the name. But leaving the paternal roof to wash other people's teacups, nurse other people's ails, and obey other people's orders for hire – this, this was degradation; and headstrong Louisa would disgrace her name forever if she did it.

Opposition only fired the revolutionary blood in my veins, and I crowned my iniquity by the rebellious declaration:

'If doing this work hurts my respectability, I wouldn't give much for it. My aristocratic ancestors don't feed or clothe me and my democratic ideas of honesty and honor won't let me be idle or dependent. You need not know me if you are ashamed of me, and I won't ask you for a penny; so, if I never do succeed in anything, I shall have the immense satisfaction of knowing I am under no obligation to anyone.'

In spite of the laughter and the lamentation, I got ready my small wardrobe, consisting of two calico dresses and one delaine, made by myself, also several large and uncompromising blue aprons and three tidy little sweeping caps; for I had some English notions about housework and felt that my muslin hair protectors would be useful in some of the 'light labors' I was to undertake. It is needless to say they were very becoming. Then, firmly embracing my family, I set forth one cold January day, with my little trunk, a stout heart, and a five-dollar bill for my fortune.

5

'She will be back in a week,' was my sister's prophecy, as she wiped her weeping eye.

'No, she won't, for she has promised to stay the month out and she will keep her word,' answered my mother, who always defended the black sheep of her flock.

I heard both speeches, and registered a tremendous vow to keep that promise, if I died in the attempt – little dreaming, poor innocent, what lay before me.

Josephus meantime had written me several remarkable letters, describing the different members of the family I was about to enter. His account was peculiar; but I believed every word of it and my romantic fancy was much excited by the details he gave. The principal ones are as follows, condensed from the voluminous epistles which he evidently enjoyed writing:

You will find a stately mansion, fast falling to decay, for my father will have nothing repaired, preferring that the old house and its master should crumble away together. I have, however, been permitted to rescue a few rooms from ruin; and here I pass my recluse life, surrounded by the things I love. This will naturally be more attractive to you than the gloomy apartments my father inhabits, and I hope you will here allow me to minister to your young and cheerful nature when your daily cares are over. I need such companionship and shall always welcome you to my abode.

Eliza, my sister, is a child at forty, for she has lived alone with my father and an old servant all her life. She is a good creature, but not lively, and needs stirring up, as you will soon see. Also I hope by your means to rescue her from the evil influence of Puah, who, in my estimation, is a *wretch*. She has gained entire control over Eliza, and warps her mind with great skill, prejudicing her against *me*, and thereby desolating my home. Puah hates *me* and always has. Why I know not, except that I will not yield to her control. She ruled here for years while I was away, and my return upset all her nefarious plans. It will always be my firm opinion that she has tried to *poison me*, and may again. But even this dark suspicion will not deter me from my duty. I cannot send her away, for both my deluded father and my sister have entire faith in her, and I cannot shake it. She is faithful and kind to them, so I submit and remain to guard them, even at the risk of my life.

I tell you these things because I wish you to know all and be warned, for this old hag has a specious tongue, and I should grieve to see you deceived by her lies. Say nothing, but watch her silently, and help me to thwart her evil plots; but do not trust her, or beware.

Now this was altogether romantic and sensational, and I felt as if about to enter one of those delightfully dangerous houses we read of in novels, where perils, mysteries, and sins freely disport themselves, till the newcomer sets all to rights, after unheard of trials and escapes.

I arrived at twilight, just the proper time for the heroine to appear; and, as no one answered my modest solo on the rusty knocker, I walked in and looked about me. Yes, here was the long, shadowy hall, where the ghosts doubtless walked at midnight. Peering in at an open door on the right, I saw a parlor full of ancient furniture, faded, dusty, and dilapidated. Old portraits stared at me from the walls and a damp chill froze the marrow of my bones in the most approved style.

'The romance opens well,' I thought, and, peeping in at an opposite door, beheld a luxurious apartment, full of the warm glow of firelight, the balmy breath of hyacinths and roses, the white glimmer of piano keys, and tempting rows of books along the walls.

The contrast between the two rooms was striking, and, after an admiring survey, I continued my explorations, thinking that I should not mind being 'ministered to' in that inviting place when my work was done.

A third door showed me a plain, dull sitting room, with an old man napping in his easy chair. I heard voices in the kitchen beyond, and, entering there, beheld Puah the fiend. Unfortunately for the dramatic effect of the tableaux, all I saw was a mild-faced old woman, buttering toast, while she conversed with her familiar, a comfortable gray cat.

The old lady greeted me kindly, but I fancied her faded blue eye had a weird expression and her amiable words were all a snare, though I own I was rather disappointed at the commonplace appearance of this humble Borgia.

She showed me to a tiny room, where I felt more like a young giantess than ever, and was obliged to stow away my possessions as snugly as in a ship's cabin. When I presently descended, armed with a blue apron and 'a heart for any fate', I found the old man awake and received from him a welcome full of ancient courtesy and kindliness. Miss Eliza crept in like a timid mouse, looking so afraid of her buxom companion that I forgot my own shyness in trying to relieve hers. She was so enveloped in shawls that all I could discover was that my mistress was a very nervous little woman, with a small button of pale hair on the outside of her head and the vaguest notions of work inside. A few spasmodic remarks and many awkward pauses brought us to teatime, when Josephus appeared, as tall, thin, and cadaverous as ever. After his arrival there was no more silence, for he preached all suppertime something in this agreeable style:

My young friend, our habits, as you see, are of the simplest. We eat in the kitchen, and all together, in the primitive fashion; for it suits my father and saves labor. I could wish more order and elegance; but *my* wishes are not consulted and I submit. I live above these petty crosses, and, though my health suffers from bad cookery, I do not murmur. Only, I must say, in passing, that if you *will* make your battercakes green with saleratus, Puah, I shall feel it my duty to throw them out of the window. *I* am used to poison; but I cannot see the coats of this blooming girl's stomach destroyed, as mine have been. And, speaking of duties, I may as well mention to you, Louisa (I call you so in a truly fraternal spirit), that I like to find my study in order when I come down in the morning; for I often need a few moments of solitude before I face the daily annoyances of my life. I shall permit *you* to perform this light task, for *you* have some idea of order (I see it in the formation of your brow), and feel sure that *you* will respect the sanctuary of thought. Eliza is so blind she does not see dust, and Puah enjoys devastating the one poor refuge I can call my own this side the grave. We are all waiting for you, sir. My father keeps up the old formalities, you observe; and I endure them, though *my* views are more advanced.

The old gentleman hastily finished his tea and returned thanks, when his son stalked gloomily away, evidently oppressed with the burden of his wrongs, also, as I irreverently fancied, with the seven 'green' flapjacks he had devoured during the sermon.

I helped wash up the cups, and during that domestic rite Puah chatted in what I should have considered a cheery, social way had I not been darkly warned against her wiles.

'You needn't mind half Josephus says, my dear. He likes to hear himself talk and always goes on so before folks. I sometimes thinks his books and new idees have sort of muddled his wits, for he is as full of notions as a paper is of pins; and he gets dreadfully put out if we don't give in to 'em. But, gracious me! they are so redicklus sometimes and so selfish I can't allow him to make a fool of himself or plague Lizy. She don't dare to say her soul is her own; so I have to stand up for her. His pa don't know half his odd doings; for I try to keep the old gentleman comfortable and have to manage 'em all, which is not an easy job, I do assure you.'

I had a secret conviction that she was right, but did not commit myself in any way, and we joined the social circle in the sitting room. The prospect was not a lively one, for the old gentleman nodded behind his newspaper; Eliza, with her head pinned up in a little blanket, slumbered on the sofa, Puah fell to knitting silently; and the plump cat dozed under the stove. Josephus was visible, artistically posed in the luxurious recesses of his cell, with the light beaming on his thoughtful brow, as he pored over a large volume or mused with upturned eye.

Having nothing else to do, I sat and stared at him, till, emerging from a deep reverie, with an effective start, he became conscious of my existence and beckoned me to approach the 'sanctuary of thought' with a melodramatic waft of his large hand.

I went, took possession of an easy chair, and prepared myself for elegant conversation. I was disappointed, however; for Josephus showed me a list of his favorite dishes, sole fruit of all that absorbing thought, and, with an earnestness that flushed his saffron countenance, gave me hints as to the proper preparation of these delicacies.

I mildly mentioned that I was not a cook; but was effectually silenced by being reminded that I came to be generally useful, to take his sister's place, and see that the flame of life which burned so feebly in this earthly tabernacle was fed with proper fuel. Mince pies, Welsh rarebits, sausages, and strong coffee did

11

not strike me as strictly spiritual fare; but I listened meekly and privately resolved to shift this awful responsibility to Puah's shoulders.

Detecting me in gape, after an hour of this high converse, he presented me with an overblown rose, which fell to pieces before I got out of the room, pressed my hand, and dismissed me with a fervent: 'God bless you, child. Don't forget the dropped eggs for breakfast.'

I was up betimes next morning and had the study in perfect order before the recluse appeared, enjoying a good prowl among the books as I worked and becoming so absorbed that I forgot the eggs, till a gusty sigh startled me, and I beheld Josephus, in dressing gown and slippers, languidly surveying the scene.

'Nay, do not fly,' he said, as I grasped my duster in guilty haste. 'It pleases me to see you here and lends a sweet, domestic charm to my solitary room. I like that graceful cap, that housewifely apron, and I beg you will wear them often; for it refreshes my eye to see something tasteful, young, and womanly about me. Eliza makes a bundle of herself and Puah is simply detestable.'

He sank languidly into a chair and closed his eyes, as if the mere thought of his enemy was too much for him. I took advantage of this momentary prostration to slip away, convulsed with laughter at the looks and words of this bald-headed sentimentalist.

After breakfast I fell to work with a will, eager

to show my powers and glad to put things to rights, for many hard jobs had evidently been waiting for a stronger arm than Puah's and a more methodical head than Eliza's.

Everything was dusty, moldy, shiftless, and neglected, except the domain of Josephus. Upstairs the paper was dropping from the walls, the ancient furniture was all more or less dilapidated, and every hole and corner was full of relics tucked away by Puah, who was a regular old magpie. Rats and mice reveled in the empty rooms and spiders wove their tapestry undisturbed, for the old man would have nothing altered or repaired and his part of the house was fast going to ruin.

I longed to have a grand 'clearing up'; but was forbidden to do more than to keep things in livable order. On the whole, it was fortunate, for I soon found that my hands would be kept busy with the realms of Josephus, whose ethereal being shrank from dust, shivered at a cold breath, and needed much cosseting with dainty food, hot fires, soft beds, and endless service, else, as he expressed it, the frail reed would break.

I regret to say that a time soon came when I felt supremely indifferent as to the breakage, and very skeptical as to the fragility of a reed that ate, slept, dawdled, and scolded so energetically. The rose that fell to pieces so suddenly was a good symbol of the rapid disappearance of all the romantic delusions I had indulged in for a time. A week's acquaintance with the

13

inmates of this old house quite settled my opinion, and further developments only confirmed it.

Miss Eliza was a nonentity and made no more impression on me than a fly. The old gentleman passed his days in a placid sort of doze and took no notice of what went on about him. Puah had been a faithful drudge for years, and, instead of being a 'wretch', was, as I soon satisfied myself, a motherly old soul, with no malice in her. The secret of Josephus's dislike was that the reverend tyrant ruled the house, and all obeyed him but Puah, who had nursed him as a baby, boxed his ears as a boy, and was not afraid of him even when he became a man and a minister. I soon repented of my first suspicions, and grew fond of her, for without my old gossip I should have fared ill when my day of tribulation came.

At first I innocently accepted the fraternal invitations to visit the study, feeling that when my day's work was done I earned a right to rest and read. But I soon found that this was not the idea. I was not to read; but to be read to. I was not to enjoy the flowers, pictures, fire, and books; but to keep them in order for my lord to enjoy. I was also to be a passive bucket, into which he was to pour all manner of philosophic, metaphysical, and sentimental rubbish. I was to serve his needs, soothe his sufferings, and sympathize with all his sorrows – be a galley slave, in fact.

As soon as I clearly understood this, I tried to put an end to it by shunning the study and never lingering there an instant after my work was done. But it availed little, for Josephus demanded much sympathy and was bound to have it. So he came and read poems while I washed dishes, discussed his pet problems all meal times, and put reproachful notes under my door, in which were comically mingled complaints of neglect and orders for dinner.

I bore it as long as I could, and then freed my mind in a declaration of independence, delivered in the kitchen, where he found me scrubbing the hearth. It was not an impressive attitude for an orator, nor was the occupation one a girl would choose when receiving calls; but I have always felt grateful for the intense discomfort of that moment, since it gave me courage to rebel outright. Stranded on a small island of mat, in a sea of soapsuds, I brandished a scrubbing brush, as I indignantly informed him that I came to be a companion to his sister, not to him, and I should keep that post or none. This I followed up by reproaching him with the delusive reports he had given me of the place and its duties, and assuring him that I should not stay long unless matters mended.

'But I offer you lighter tasks, and you refuse them,' he begun, still hovering in the doorway, whither he had hastily retired when I opened my batteries.

'But I don't like the tasks, and consider them much worse than hard work,' was my ungrateful answer, as I sat upon my island, with the soft soap conveniently near.

'Do you mean to say you prefer to scrub that hearth to sitting in my charming room while I read Hegel to you?' he demanded, glaring down upon me.

'Infinitely,' I responded promptly, and emphasized my words by beginning to scrub with a zeal that made the bricks white with foam.

'Is it possible!' and, with a groan at my depravity, Josephus retired, full of ungodly wrath.

I remember that I immediately burst into jocund song, so that no doubt might remain in his mind, and continued to warble cheerfully till my task was done. I also remember that I cried heartily when I got to my room, I was so vexed, disappointed, and tired. But my bower was so small I should soon have swamped the furniture if I had indulged copiously in tears; therefore I speedily dried them up, wrote a comic letter home, and waited with interest to see what would happen next.

Far be it from me to accuse one of the nobler sex of spite or the small revenge of underhand annoyances and slights to one who could not escape and would not retaliate; but after that day a curious change came over the spirit of that very unpleasant dream. Gradually all the work of the house had been slipping into my hands; for Eliza was too poorly to help or direct, and Puah too old to do much besides the cooking. About this time I found that even the roughest work was added to my share, for Josephus was unusually feeble and no one was hired to do his chores. Having made up my mind to go when the month was out, I said nothing, but dug

16

paths, brought water from the well, split kindlings, made fires, and sifted ashes, like a true Cinderella.

There never had been any pretense of companionship with Eliza, who spent her days mulling over the fire, and seldom exerted herself except to find odd jobs for me to do – rusty knives to clean, sheets to turn, old stockings to mend, and, when all else failed, some paradise of moths and mice to be cleared up; for the house was full of such 'glory holes'.

If I remonstrated, Eliza at once dissolved into tears and said she must do as she was told; Puah begged me to hold on till spring, when things would be much better; and pity pleaded for the two poor souls. But I don't think I could have stood it if my promise had not bound me, for when the fiend said 'Budge' honor said 'Budge not', and I stayed.

But, being a mortal worm, I turned now and then when the ireful Josephus trod upon me too hard, especially in the matter of boot-blacking. I really don't know why that is considered such humiliating work for a woman; but so it is, and there I drew the line. I would have cleaned the old man's shoes without a murmur; but he preferred to keep their native rustiness intact. Eliza never went out, and Puah affected carpet slippers of the Chinese-junk pattern. Josephus, however, plumed himself upon his feet, which, like his nose, were large, and never took his walks abroad without having his boots in a high state of polish. He had brushed them himself at first; but soon after the explosion I discovered a pair

17

of muddy boots in the shed, set suggestively near the blacking box. I did not take the hint, feeling instinctively that this amiable being was trying how much I would bear for the sake of peace.

The boots remained untouched; and another pair soon came to keep them company, whereat I smiled wickedly as I chopped just kindlings enough for my own use. Day after day the collection grew, and neither party gave in. Boots were succeeded by shoes, then rubbers gave a pleasing variety to the long line, and then I knew the end was near.

'Why are not my boots attended to?' demanded Josephus, one evening, when obliged to go out.

'I'm sure I don't know,' was Eliza's helpless answer.

'I told Louizy I guessed you'd want some of 'em before long,' observed Puah, with an exasperating twinkle in her old eye.

'And what did she say?' asked my lord with an ireful whack of his velvet slippers as he cast them down.

'Oh! She said she was so busy doing your other work you'd have to do that yourself; and I thought she was about right.'

'Louizy' heard it all through the slide, and could have embraced the old woman for her words, but kept still till Josephus had resumed his slippers with a growl and retired to the shed, leaving Eliza in tears, Puah chuckling, and the rebellious handmaid exulting in the china closet.

Alas! For romance and the Christian virtues,

18

several pairs of boots were cleaned that night, and my sinful soul enjoyed the spectacle of the reverend boot-black at his task. I even found my 'fancy work', as I called the evening job of paring a bucketful of hard russets with a dull knife, much cheered by the shoe brush accompaniment played in the shed.

Thunder clouds rested upon the martyr's brow at breakfast, and I was as much ignored as the cat. And what a relief that was! The piano was locked up, so were the bookcases, the newspapers mysteriously disappeared, and a solemn silence reigned at table, for no one dared to talk when that gifted tongue was mute. Eliza fled from the gathering storm and had a comfortable fit of neuralgia in her own room, where Puah nursed her, leaving me to skirmish with the enemy.

It was not a fair fight, and that experience lessened my respect for mankind immensely. I did my best, however – grubbed about all day and amused my dreary evenings as well as I could; too proud even to borrow a book, lest it should seem like a surrender. What a long month it was, and how eagerly I counted the hours of that last week, for my time was up Saturday, and I hoped to be off at once. But when I announced my intention such dismay fell upon Eliza that my heart was touched, and Puah so urgently begged me to stay till they could get some one that I consented to remain a few days longer, and wrote post-haste to my mother, telling her to send a substitute quickly or I should do something desperate.

That blessed woman, little dreaming of all the woes I had endured, advised me to be patient, to do the generous thing, and be sure I should not regret it in the end. I groaned, submitted, and did regret it all the days of my life.

Three mortal weeks I waited; for, though two other victims came, I was implored to set them going, and tried to do it. But both fled after a day or two, condemning the place as a very hard one and calling me a fool to stand it another hour. I entirely agreed with them on both points, and, when I had cleared up after the second incapable lady, I tarried not for the coming of a third, but clutched my property and announced my departure by the next train.

Of course, Eliza wept, Puah moaned, the old man politely regretted, and the younger one washed his hands of the whole affair by shutting himself up in his room and forbidding me to say farewell because he 'could not bear it.' I laughed, and fancied it done for effect then; but I soon understood it better and did not laugh.

At the last moment, Eliza nervously tucked a six-penny pocketbook into my hand and shrouded herself in the little blanket with a sob. But Puah kissed me kindly and whispered, with an odd look: 'Don't blame us for anything. Some folks is liberal and some ain't.' I thanked the poor old soul for her kindness to me and trudged gayly away to the station, whither my property had preceded me on a wheelbarrow, hired at my own expense.

I never shall forget that day. A bleak March afternoon, a sloppy, lonely road, and one hoarse crow stalking about a field, so like Josephus that I could not resist throwing a snowball at him. Behind me stood the dull old house, no longer either mysterious or romantic in my disenchanted eyes; before me rumbled the barrow, bearing my dilapidated wardrobe; and in my pocket reposed what I fondly hoped was, if not a liberal, at least an honest return for seven weeks of the hardest work I ever did.

Unable to resist the desire to see what my earnings were, I opened the purse and beheld *four dollars.*

I have had a good many bitter minutes in my life; but one of the bitterest came to me as I stood there in the windy road, with the sixpenny pocketbook open before me, and looked from my poor chapped, grimy, chill-blained hands to the paltry sum that was considered reward enough for all the hard and humble labor they had done.

A girl's heart is a sensitive thing. And mine had been very full lately; for it had suffered many of the trials that wound deeply yet cannot be told; so I think it was but natural that my first impulse was to go straight back to that sacred study and fling this insulting money at the feet of him who sent it. But I was so boiling over with indignation that I could not trust myself in his presence, lest I should be unable to resist the temptation to shake him, in spite of his cloth.

No, I would go home, show my honorable wounds,

tell my pathetic tale, and leave my parents to avenge my wrongs. I did so; but over that harrowing scene I drop a veil, for my feeble pen refuses to depict the emotions of my outraged family. I will merely mention that the four dollars went back and the Reverend Josephus never heard the last of it in that neighborhood.

My experiment seemed a dire failure and I mourned it as such for years; but more than once in my life I have been grateful for that serio-comico experience, since it has taught me many lessons. One of the most useful of these has been the power of successfully making a companion, not a servant, of those whose aid I need, and helping to gild their honest wages with the sympathy and justice which can sweeten the humblest and lighten the hardest task.

– Transcendental Wild Oats –
(1873)

On the first day of June, 184–, a large wagon, drawn by a small horse and containing a motley load, went lumbering over certain New England hills, with the pleasing accompaniments of wind, rain, and hail. A serene man with a serene child upon his knee was driving, or rather being driven, for the small horse had it all his own way. A brown boy with a William Penn style of countenance sat beside him, firmly embracing a bust of Socrates. Behind them was an energetic-looking woman, with a benevolent brow, satirical mouth, and eyes brimful of hope and courage. A baby reposed upon her lap, a mirror leaned against her knee, and a basket of provisions danced about at her feet, as she struggled with a large, unruly umbrella. Two blue-eyed little girls, with hands full of childish treasures, sat under one old shawl, chatting happily together.

In front of this lively party stalked a tall, sharp-featured man, in a long blue cloak; and a fourth small girl trudged alone beside him through the mud as if she rather enjoyed it.

The wind whistled over the bleak hills; the rain fell in a despondent drizzle, and twilight began to fall. But the calm man gazed as tranquilly into the fog as if he beheld a radiant bow of promise spanning the gray sky. The cheery woman tried to cover everyone but herself with the big umbrella. The brown boy pillowed his head on the bald pate of Socrates and slumbered peacefully. The little girls sang lullabies to their dolls in soft, maternal murmurs. The sharp-nosed pedestrian marched steadily on, with the blue cloak streaming out behind him like a banner; and the lively infant splashed through the puddles with a duck-like satisfaction pleasant to behold.

Thus these modern pilgrims journeyed hopefully out of the old world, to found a new one in the wilderness . . .

This prospective Eden at present consisted of an old red farmhouse, a dilapidated barn, many acres of meadowland, and a grove. Ten ancient apple trees were all the 'chaste supply' which the place offered as yet; but, in the firm belief that plenteous orchards were soon to be evoked from their inner consciousness, these sanguine founders had christened their domain Fruitlands.

Here Timon Lion intended to found a colony of Latter Day Saints, who, under his patriarchal sway, should regenerate the world and glorify his name for ever. Here Abel Lamb, with the devoutest faith in the high ideal which was to him a living truth, desired to plant a Paradise, where Beauty, Virtue, Justice, and Love might live happily together, without the possibility of a serpent entering in. And here his wife, unconverted but faithful to the end, hoped, after many wanderings over the face of the earth, to find rest for herself and a home for her children.

'There is our new abode,' announced the enthusiast, smiling with a satisfaction quite undamped by the drops dripping from his hat brim, as they turned at length into a cart path that wound along a steep hillside into a barren looking valley.

'A little difficult of access,' observed his practical wife, as she endeavored to keep her various household goods from going overboard with every lurch of the laden ark.

'Like all good things. But those who earnestly desire and patiently seek will soon find us,' placidly responded the philosopher from the mud, through which he was now endeavoring to pilot the much enduring horse.

'Truth lies at the bottom of a well, Sister Hope,' said Brother Timon, pausing to detach his small comrade from a gate, whereon she was perched for a clearer gaze into futurity.

'That's the reason we so seldom get at it, I suppose,' replied Mrs Hope, making a vain clutch at the mirror, which a sudden jolt sent flying out of her hands.

'We want no false reflections here,' said Timon, with a grim smile, as he crunched the fragments under foot in his onward march.

Sister Hope held her peace, and looked wistfully through the mist at her promised home. The old red house with a hospitable glimmer at its windows cheered her eyes; and, considering the weather, was a fitter refuge than the sylvan bowers some of the more ardent souls might have preferred.

The newcomers were welcomed by one of the elect precious: a regenerate farmer, whose idea of reform consisted chiefly in wearing white cotton raiment and shoes of untanned leather. This costume, with a snowy beard, gave him a venerable, and at the same time a somewhat bridal appearance.

The goods and chattels of the Society not having arrived, the weary family reposed before the fire on blocks of wood, while Brother Moses White regaled them with roasted potatoes, brown bread and water, in two plates, a tin pan, and one mug; his table service being limited. But, having cast the forms and vanities of a depraved world behind them, the elders welcomed hardship with the enthusiasm of new pioneers, and the children heartily enjoyed this foretaste of what they believed was to be a sort of perpetual picnic.

During the progress of this frugal meal, two more brothers appeared. One was a dark, melancholy man, clad in homespun, whose peculiar mission was to turn his name hind part before and use as few words as possible. The other was a bland, bearded Englishman, who expected to be saved by eating uncooked food and going without clothes. He had not yet adopted the primitive costume, however; but contented himself with meditatively chewing dry beans out of a basket.

'Every meal should be a sacrament, and the vessels used should be beautiful and symbolical,' observed Brother Lamb, mildly, righting the tin pan slipping about on his knees. 'I priced a silver service when in town, but it was too costly; so I got some graceful cups and vases of Britannia ware.'

'Hardest things in the world to keep bright. Will whiting be allowed in the community?' inquired Sister Hope, with a housewife's interest in labor-saving institutions.

'Such trivial questions will be discussed at a more fitting time,' answered Brother Timon, sharply, as he burnt his fingers with a very hot potato. 'Neither sugar, molasses, milk, butter, cheese, nor flesh are to be used among us, for nothing is to be admitted which has caused wrong or death to man or beast.'

'Our garments are to be linen till we learn to raise our own cotton or some substitute for woolen fabrics,' added Brother Abel, blissfully basking in an imaginary future as warm and brilliant as the generous fire before him.

'Haou abaout shoes!' asked Brother Moses, surveying his own with interest.

'We must yield that point till we can manufacture an innocent substitute for leather. Bark, wood, or some durable fabric will be invented in time. Meanwhile, those who desire to carry out our idea to the fullest extent can go barefooted,' said Lion, who liked extreme measures.

'I never will, nor let my girls,' murmured rebellious Sister Hope, under her breath.

'Haou do you cattle'ate to treat the ten-acre lot! Ef things ain't 'tended to right smart, we shan't hev no crops,' observed the practical patriarch in cotton.

'We shall spade it,' replied Abel, in such perfect good faith that Moses said no more, though he indulged in a shake of the head as he glanced at hands that had held nothing heavier than a pen for years. He was a paternal old soul and regarded the younger men as promising boys on a new sort of lark.

'What shall we do for lamps, if we cannot use any animal substance! I do hope light of some sort is to be thrown upon the enterprise,' said Mrs Lamb, with anxiety, for in those days kerosene and camphene were not, and gas unknown in the wilderness.

'We shall go without till we have discovered some vegetable oil or wax to serve us,' replied Brother Timon, in a decided tone, which caused Sister Hope to resolve that her private lamp should be always trimmed, if not burning.

'Each member is to perform the work for which experience, strength, and taste best fit him,' continued Dictator Lion. 'Thus drudgery and disorder will be avoided and harmony prevail. We shall rise at dawn, begin the day by bathing, followed by music, and then a chaste repast of fruit and bread. Each one finds congenial occupation till the meridian meal; when some deep-searching conversation gives rest to the body and development to the mind. Healthful labor again engages us till the last meal, when we assemble in social communion, prolonged till sunset, when we retire to sweet repose, ready for the next day's activity.'

'What part of the work do you incline to yourself?' asked Sister Hope, with a humorous glimmer in her keen eyes.

'I shall wait till it is made clear to me. Being in preference to doing is the great aim, and this comes to us rather by a resigned willingness than a wilful activity, which is a check to all divine growth,' responded Brother Timon.

'I thought so.' And Mrs Lamb sighed audibly, for during the year he had spent in her family Brother Timon had so faithfully carried out his idea of 'being, not doing', that she had found his 'divine growth' both an expensive and unsatisfactory process.

Here her husband struck into the conversation, his face shining with the light and joy of the splendid dreams and high ideals hovering before him.

'In these steps of reform, we do not rely so much on scientific reasoning or physiological skill as on the spirit's dictates. The greater part of man's duty consists in leaving alone much that he now does. Shall I stimulate with tea, coffee, or wine! No. Shall I consume flesh! Not if I value health. Shall I subjugate cattle! Shall I claim property in any created thing! Shall I trade! Shall I adopt a form of religion! Shall I interest myself in politics! To how many of these questions –

could we ask them deeply enough and could they be heard as having relation to our eternal welfare – would the response be 'Abstain'!'

A mild snore seemed to echo the last word of Abel's rhapsody, for Brother Moses had succumbed to mundane slumber and sat nodding like a massive ghost. Forest Absalom, the silent man, and John Pease, the English member, now departed to the barn; and Mrs Lamb led her flock to a temporary fold, leaving the founders of the 'Consociate Family' to build castles in the air till the fire went out and the symposium ended in smoke.

The furniture arrived next day, and was soon bestowed; for the principal property of the community consisted in books. To this rare library was devoted the best room in the house, and the few busts and pictures that still survived many nittings were added to beautify the sanctuary, for here the family was to meet for amusement, instruction, and worship.

Any housewife can imagine the emotions of Sister Hope, when she took possession of a large, dilapidated kitchen, containing an old stove and the peculiar stores out of which food was to be evolved for her little family of eleven. Cakes of maple sugar, dried peas and beans, barley and hominy, meal of all sorts, potatoes, and dried fruit. No milk, butter, cheese, tea, or meat appeared. Even salt was considered a useless luxury and spice entirely forbidden by these lovers of Spartan simplicity. A ten years' experience of vegetarian vagaries had been good training for this new freak, and her sense of the ludicrous supported her through many trying scenes.

Unleavened bread, porridge, and water for breakfast; bread, vegetables, and water for dinner; bread, fruit, and water for supper was the bill of fare ordained by the elders. No teapot profaned that sacred stove, no gory steak cried aloud for vengeance from her chaste gridiron; and only a brave woman's taste, time, and temper were sacrificed on that domestic altar.

The vexed question of light was settled by buying a quantity of bayberry wax for candles; and, on discovering that no one knew how to make them, pine knots were introduced, to be used when absolutely necessary. Being summer, the evenings were not long, and the weary fraternity found it no great hardship to retire with the birds. The inner light was sufficient for most of them. But Mrs Lamb rebelled. Evening was the only time she had to herself, and while the tired feet rested the skillful hands mended torn frocks and little stockings, or anxious heart forgot its burden in a book.

So 'Mother's lamp' burned steadily, while the philosophers built a new heaven and earth by moonlight; and through all the metaphysical mists and philanthropic pyrotechnics of that period Sister Hope played her own little game of 'throwing light', and none but the moths were the worse for it.

Such farming probably was never seen before since Adam delved. The band of brothers began by spading garden and field; but a few days of it lessened their ardor amazingly. Blistered hands and aching backs suggested the expediency of permitting the use of cattle till the workers were better fitted for noble toil by a summer of the new life.

Brother Moses brought a yoke of oxen from his farm, at least, the philosophers thought so till it was discovered that one of the animals was a cow; and Moses confessed that he 'must be let down easy, for he couldn't live on garden sarse entirely.'

Great was Dictator Lion's indignation at this lapse from virtue. But time pressed, the work must be done; so the meek cow was permitted to wear the yoke and the recreant brother continued to enjoy forbidden draughts in the barn, which dark proceeding caused the children to regard him as one set apart for destruction.

The sowing was equally peculiar, for, owing to some mistake, the three brethren, who devoted themselves to this graceful task, found when about half through the job that each had been sowing a different sort of grain in the same field; a mistake which caused much perplexity, as it could not be remedied; but, after a long consultation and a good deal of laughter, it was decided to say nothing and see what would come of it.

The garden was planted with a generous supply of useful roots and herbs; but, as manure was not allowed to profane the virgin soil, few of these vegetable treasures ever came up. Purslanes reigned supreme, and the disappointed planters ate it philosophically, deciding that Nature knew what was best for them, and would generously supply their needs, if they could only learn to digest her 'sallets' and wild roots.

The orchard was laid out, a little grafting done, new trees and vines set, regardless of the unfit season and entire ignorance of the husbandmen, who honestly believed that in the autumn they would reap a bounteous harvest.

Slowly things got into order, and rapidly rumors of the new experiment went abroad, causing many strange spirits to knock thither, for in those days communities were the fashion and transcendentalism raged wildly. Some came to look on and laugh, some to be supported in poetic idleness, a few to believe sincerely and work heartily. Each member was allowed to mount his favorite hobby and ride it to his heart's content. Very queer were some of the riders, and very rampant some of the hobbies.

One youth, believing that language was of little consequence if the spirit was only right, startled newcomers by blandly greeting them with 'Good morning, damn you,' and other remarks of an equally mixed order. A second irrepressible being held that all the emotions of the soul should be freely expressed, and illustrated his theory by antics that would have sent him to a lunatic asylum, if, as an unregenerate wag said, he had not already been in one. When his spirit soared, he climbed trees and shouted; when doubt assailed him, he lay upon the floor and groaned lamentably. At joyful periods, he raced, leaped, and sang; when sad, he wept aloud; and when a great thought burst upon him in the watches of the night, he crowed like a jocund cockerel, to the great delight of the children and the great annoyance of the elders. One musical brother fiddled whenever so moved, sang sentimentally to the four little girls, and put a music box on the wall when he hoed corn.

Brother Pease ground away at his uncooked food, or browsed over the farm on sorrel, mint, green fruit, and new vegetables. Occasionally he took his walks abroad, airily attired in an unbleached cotton poncho, which was the nearest approach to the primeval costume he was allowed to indulge in. At midsummer he retired to the wilderness, to try his plan where the woodchucks were without prejudices and huckleberry bushes were hospitably full. A sunstroke unfortunately spoilt his plan, and he returned to semi-civilization a sadder and wiser man.

Forest Absalom preserved his Pythagorean silence, cultivated his fine dark locks, and worked like a beaver, setting an excellent example of brotherly love, justice, and fidelity by his upright life. He it was who helped overworked Sister Hope with her heavy washes, kneaded the endless succession of batches of bread, watched over the children, and did the many tasks left undone by the brethren, who were so busy discussing and defining great duties that they forgot to perform the small ones.

Moses White placidly plodded about, 'chorin' around', as he called it, looking like an old-time patriarch, with his silver hair and flowing beard, and saving the community from many a mishap by his thrift and Yankee shrewdness.

Brother Lion domineered over the whole concern; for, having put the most money into the speculation, he was resolved to make it pay: as if anything founded on an ideal basis could be expected to do so by any but enthusiasts.

Abel Lamb simply reveled in the Newness, firmly believing that his dream was to be beautifully realized and in time not only little Fruitlands, but the whole earth, be turned into a Happy Valley. He worked with every muscle of his body, for he was in deadly earnest. He taught with his whole head and heart; planned and sacrificed, preached and prophesied, with a soul full of the purest aspirations, most unselfish purposes, and desires for a life devoted to God and man, too high and tender to bear the rough usage of this world.

It was a little remarkable that only one woman ever joined this community. Mrs Lamb merely followed wheresoever her husband led: 'as ballast for his balloon,' as she said, in her bright way.

Miss Jane Gage was a stout lady of mature years, sentimental, amiable, and lazy. She wrote verses copiously, and had vague yearnings and graspings after the unknown, which led her to believe herself fitted for a higher sphere than any she had yet adorned.

Having been a teacher, she was set to instructing the children in the common branches. Each adult member took a turn at the infants; and, as each taught in his own way, the result was a chronic state of chaos in the minds of these much-afflicted innocents.

Sleep, food, and poetic musings were the desires of dear Jane's life, and she shirked all duties as clogs upon her spirit's wings. Any thought of lending a hand with the domestic drudgery never occurred to her; and when to the question, 'Are there any beasts of burden on the place?' Mrs Lamb answered, with a face that told its own tale, 'Only one woman!' the buxom Jane took no shame to herself, but laughed at the joke, and let the stout-hearted sister tug on alone.

Unfortunately, the poor lady hankered after the fleshpots, and endeavored to stay herself with private sips of milk, crackers, and cheese, and on one dire occasion she partook of fish at a neighbor's table.

One of the children reported this sad lapse from virtue, and poor Jane was publicly reprimanded by Timon.

'I only took a little bit of the tail,' sobbed the penitent poetess.

'Yes, but the whole fish had to be tortured and slain that you might tempt your carnal appetite with that one taste of the tail. Know ye not, consumers of flesh meat, that ye are nourishing the wolf and tiger in your bosoms?'

At this awful question and the peal of laughter

which arose from some of the younger brethren, tickled by the ludicrous contrast between the stout sinner, the stern judge, and the naughty satisfaction of the young detective, poor Jane fled from the room to pack her trunk and return to the world where fishes' tails were not forbidden fruit.

Transcendental wild oats were sown broadcast that year, and the fame thereof has not yet ceased in the land; for, futile as this crop seemed to outsiders, it bore an invisible harvest, worth much to those who planted in earnest. As none of the members of this particular community have ever recounted their experiences before, a few of them may not be amiss, since the interest in these attempts has never died out and Fruitlands was the most ideal of all these castles in Spain.

A new dress was invented, since cotton, silk, and wool were forbidden as the product of slave labor, worm slaughter, and sheep-robbery. Tunics and trousers of brown linen were the only wear. The women's skirts were longer, and their straw hat brims wider than the men's, and this was the only difference. Some persecution lent a charm to the costume, and the long-haired, linen-clad reformers quite enjoyed the mild martyrdom they endured when they left home.

Money was abjured, as the root of all evil. The produce of the land was to supply most of their wants, or be exchanged for the few things they could not grow. This idea had its inconveniences; but self-denial was the fashion, and it was surprising how many things one can do without. When they desired to travel, they walked, if possible, begged the loan of a vehicle, or boldly entered car or coach, and, stating their principles to the officials, took the consequences. Usually their dress, their earnest frankness, and gentle resolution won them a passage; but now and then they met with hard usage, and had the satisfaction of suffering for their principles.

On one of these penniless pilgrimages they took passage on a boat, and, when fare was demanded, artlessly offered to talk, instead of pay. As the boat was well under way and they actually had not a cent, there was no help for it. So Brothers Lion and Lamb held forth to the assembled passengers in their most eloquent style. There must have been something effective in this conversation, for the listeners were moved to take up a contribution for these inspired lunatics, who preached peace on earth and good will to man so earnestly, with empty pockets. A goodly sum was collected; but when the captain presented it the reformers proved that they were consistent even in their madness, for not a penny would they accept, saying, with a look at the group about them, whose indifference or contempt had changed to interest and respect: 'You see how well we get on without money'; and so went serenely on their way, with their linen blouses flapping airily in the cold October wind.

They preached vegetarianism everywhere and resisted all temptations of the flesh, contentedly eating apples and bread at well-spread tables, and much afflicting hospitable hostesses by denouncing their food and taking away their appetites, discussing the 'horrors of shambles', the 'incorporation of the brute in man', and 'on elegant abstinence the sign of a pure soul'. But, when the perplexed or offended ladies asked what they should eat, they got in reply a bill of fare consisting of 'bowls of sunrise for breakfast', 'solar seeds of the sphere', 'dishes from Plutarch's chaste table', and other viands equally hard to find in any modern market.

Reform conventions of all sorts were haunted by these brethren, who said many wise things and did many foolish ones. Unfortunately, these wanderings interfered with their harvest at home; but the rule was to do what the spirit moved, so they left their crops to Providence and went a-reaping in wider and, let us hope, more fruitful fields than their own.

Luckily, the earthly providence who watched over Abel Lamb was at hand to glean the scanty crop yielded by the 'uncorrupted land', which, 'consecrated to human freedom', had received 'the sober culture of devout men'.

About the time the grain was ready to house, some call of the Oversoul wafted all the men away. An easterly storm was coming up and the yellow stacks were sure to be ruined. Then Sister Hope gathered her forces. Three little girls, one boy (Timon's son), and herself, harnessed to clothes baskets and Russia-linen sheets, were the only teams she could command; but with these poor appliances the indomitable woman got in the grain and saved food for her young, with the instinct and energy of a mother bird with a brood of hungry nestlings to feed.

This attempt at regeneration had its tragic as well as comic side, though the world only saw the former.

With the first frosts, the butterflies, who had sunned themselves in the new light through the summer, took flight, leaving the few bees to see what honey they had stored for winter use. Precious little appeared beyond the satisfaction of a few months of holy living.

At first it seemed as if a chance to try holy dying also was to be offered them. Timon, much disgusted with the failure of the scheme, decided to retire to the Shakers, who seemed to be the only successful community going.

'What is to become of us!' asked Mrs Hope, for Abel was heartbroken at the bursting of his lovely bubble.

'You can stay here, if you like, till a tenant is found. No more wood must be cut, however, and no more corn ground. All I have must be sold to pay the debts of the concern, as the responsibility rests with me,' was the cheering reply.

'Who is to pay us for what we have lost! I gave all I had – furniture, time, strength, six months of my children's lives – and all are wasted. Abel gave himself body and soul, and is almost wrecked by hard work and disappointment. Are we to have no return for this, but leave to starve and freeze in an old house, with winter at hand, no money, and hardly a friend left; for this wild scheme has alienated nearly all we had. You talk much about justice. Let us have a little, since there is nothing else left.'

But the woman's appeal met with no reply but the old one: 'It was an experiment. We all risked something, and must bear our losses as we can.'

With this cold comfort, Timon departed with his son, and was absorbed into the Shaker brotherhood, where he soon found the order of things reversed, and it was all work and no play.

Then the tragedy began for the forsaken little family. Desolation and despair fell upon Abel. As his wife said, his new beliefs had alienated many friends. Some thought him mad, some unprincipled. Even the most kindly thought him a visionary, whom it was useless to help till he took more practical views of life. All stood aloof, saying: 'Let him work out his own ideas, and see what they are worth.'

He had tried, but it was a failure. The world was not ready for Utopia yet, and those who attempted to found it only got laughed at for their pains. In other days, men could sell all and give to the poor, lead lives devoted to holiness and high thought, and, after the persecution was over, find themselves honored as saints or martyrs. But in modern times these things are out of fashion. To live for one's principles, at all costs, is a dangerous speculation; and the failure of an ideal, no matter how humane and noble, is harder for the world to forgive and forget than bank robbery or the grand swindles of corrupt politicians.

Deep waters now for Abel, and for a time there seemed no passage through. Strength and spirits were exhausted by hard work and too much thought. Courage failed when, looking about for help, he saw no sympathizing face, no hand outstretched to help him, no voice to say cheerily:

'We all make mistakes, and it takes many experiences to shape a life. Try again, and let us help you.'

Every door was closed, every eye averted, every heart cold, and no way open whereby he might earn bread for his children. His principles would not permit him to do many things that others did; and in the few fields where conscience would allow him to work, who would employ a man who had flown in the face of society, as he had done?

. . . 'Hope' was the watchword now; and, while the last logs blazed on the hearth, the last bread and apples covered the table, the new commander, with recovered courage, said to her husband: 'Leave all to God – and me. He has done his part, now I will do mine.'

'But we have no money, dear.'

'Yes, we have. I sold all we could spare, and have enough to take us away from this snowbank.'

'Where can we go?'

'I have engaged four rooms at our good neighbor, Lovejoy's. There we can live cheaply till spring. Then for new plans and a home of our own, please God.'

'But, Hope, your little store won't last long, and we have no friends.'

'I can sew and you can chop wood. Lovejoy offers you the same pay as he gives his other men; my old friend, Mrs Truman, will send me all the work I want; and my blessed brother stands by us to the end. Cheer up, dear heart, for while there is work and love in the world we shall not suffer.'

'And while I have my good angel Hope, I shall not despair, even if I wait another thirty years before I step beyond the circle of the sacred little world in which I still have a place to fill.'

So one bleak December day, with their few possessions piled on an ox sled, the rosy children perched atop, and the parents trudging arm in arm behind, the exiles left their Eden and faced the world again.

'Ah, me! My happy dream. How much I leave behind that never can be mine again,' said Abel, looking back at the lost Paradise, lying white and chill in its shroud of snow.

'Yes, dear; but how much we bring away,' answered brave-hearted Hope, glancing from husband to children.

'Poor Fruitlands! The name was as great a failure as the rest!' continued Abel, with a sigh, as a frost-bitten apple fell from a leafless bough at his feet.

43

But the sigh changed to a smile as his wife added, in a half-tender, half-satirical tone: 'Don't you think Apple Slump would be a better name for it, dear!'

– *from* Sketch of Childhood –
(1898)

Running away was one of the delights of my early days; and I still enjoy sudden flights out of the nest to look about this very interesting world, and then go back to report.

On one of these occasions I passed a varied day with some Irish children, who hospitably shared their cold potatoes, salt fish, and crusts with me as we reveled in the ash heaps which then adorned the waste lands where the Albany Depot now stands. A trip to the Common cheered the afternoon, but as dusk set in and my friends deserted me, I felt that home was a nice place after all, and tried to find it. I dimly remember watching a lamp lighter as I sat to rest on some doorsteps in Bedford Street, where a big dog welcomed me so kindly that I fell asleep with my head pillowed on his curly back, and was found there by the town crier, whom my distracted parents had sent in search of me. His bell and proclamation of the loss of 'a little girl, six-years-old, in a pink frock, white hat, and new green shoes,' woke me up . . .

Being with difficulty torn from my four-footed friend, I was carried to the crier's house, and there feasted sumptuously on bread and molasses in a tin plate with the alphabet round it. But my fun ended next day when I was tied to the arm of the sofa to repent at leisure.

. . . I never went to school except to my father or such governesses as from time to time came into the family. Schools then were not what they are now; so we had lessons each morning in the study. And very happy hours they were to us, for my father taught in the wise way which unfolds what lies in the child's nature, as a flower blooms, rather than crammed it, like a Strasburg goose, with more than it could digest. I never liked arithmetic nor grammar, and dodged those branches on all occasions; but reading, writing, composition, history, and geography I enjoyed, as well as the stories read to us with a skill peculiarly his own.

Pilgrim's Progress, Krummacher's *Parables*, Miss Edgeworth, and the best of the dear old fairy tales made the reading hour the pleasantest of our day. On Sundays we had a simple service of Bible stories, hymns, and conversation about the state of our consciences and the conduct of our childish lives which never will be forgotten.

Walks each morning round the Common while in the city, and long tramps over hill and dale when our home was in the country, were a part of our education, as well as every sort of housework, for which I have always been very grateful, since such knowledge makes one independent . . . Needlework began early, and at ten my skillful sister made a linen shirt beautifully;

while at twelve I set up as a doll's dressmaker, with my sign out and wonderful models in my window. All the children employed me, and my turbans were the rage at one time, to the great dismay of the neighbors' hens, who were hotly hunted down, that I might tweak out their downiest feathers to adorn the dolls' headgear . . .

Active exercise was my delight, from the time when a child of six I drove my hoop round the Common without stopping, to the days when I did my twenty miles in five hours and went to a party in the evening.

I must have been a deer or a horse in some former state, because it was such a joy to run. No boy could be my friend till I had beaten him in a race, and no girl if she refused to climb trees, leap fences, and be a tomboy.

My wise mother, anxious to give me a strong body to support a lively brain, turned me loose in the country and let me run wild, learning of Nature what no books can teach, and being led – as those who truly love her seldom fail to be – 'Through Nature up to Nature's God.'

I remember running over the hills just at dawn one summer morning, and pausing to rest in the silent woods, saw, through an arch of trees, the sun rise over river, hill, and wide green meadows as I never saw it before.

Something born of the lovely hour, a happy mood, and the unfolding aspirations of a child's soul seemed to bring me very near to God . . . never to change through forty years of life's vicissitudes, but to grow stronger for the sharp discipline of poverty and pain, sorrow and success.

– *from* Letters from Dinan –
(1870)

We went to drive in a basket chair, very fine, with a perch behind and a smart harness; but most of the horses here are stallions, and act like time. Ours went very well at first, but in the town took to cutting up, and suddenly pounced on to a pile of brush, and stuck his head into a bake shop. We tried to get him out, but he only danced and neighed, and all the horses in town seemed to reply. A man came and led him on a bit, but he didn't mean to go, and whisked over to the other side, where he tangled us and himself up with a long string of team horses. I flew out and May soon followed. A. was driving, and kept in while the man led the 'critter' back to the stable. I declined my drive with the insane beast, and so we left him and bundled home in the most ignominious manner. All the animals are very queer here, and, unlike ours, excessively big.

We went to a ruin one day, and were about to explore the castle, when a sow, with her family of twelve, charged through the gateway at us so fiercely that we fled in dismay; for pigs are not nice when they attack . . . I flew over a hedge; May tried to follow. I pulled her over headfirst, and we tumbled into the tower like a routed garrison. It wasn't a nice ruin, but we were

49

bound to see it, having suffered so much. And we did see it, in spite of the pigs, who waylaid us on all sides, and squealed in triumph when we left, dirty, torn, and tired. The ugly things wander at their own sweet will, and are tall, round-backed, thin wretches, who run like racehorses, and are no respecters of persons.

Sunday was a great day here, for the children were confirmed. It was a pretty sight to see the long procession of little girls, in white gowns and veils, winding through the flowery garden and the antique square, into the old church, with their happy mothers following, and the boys in their church robes singing as they went. The old priest was too ill to perform the service, but the young one who did announced afterward that if the children would pass the house the old man would bless them from his bed. So all marched away down the street, with crosses and candles, and it was very touching to see the feeble old man stretch out his hands above them as the little white birds passed by with bended heads, while the fresh, boyish voices chanted the responses.

– *from* Women of Brittany –
(1870)

C lose by was a clean, rosy old woman, whose unusual occupation attracted our spinster's attention. Whisking off the wheels of a *diligence*, the old lady greased them one by one, and put them on again with the skill and speed of a regular blacksmith, and then began to pile many parcels into a *char* apparently waiting for them.

She was a brisk, cheery old soul, with the color of a winter apple in her face, plenty of fire in her quick black eyes, and a mouthful of fine teeth, though she must have been sixty. She was dressed in the costume of the place: a linen cap with several sharp gables to it, a gay kerchief over her shoulders, a blue woolen gown short enough to display a pair of sturdy feet and legs in neat shoes with bunches of ribbons on the instep and black hose. A gray apron, with pockets and a bib, finished her off; making a very sensible as well as picturesque costume.

She was still hard at it when a big boy appeared, and began to heave the trunks into another *char*; but gave out at the second, which was large. Instantly the brisk old woman put him aside, hoisted in the big boxes without help, and, catching up the shafts of the heavily laden cart, trotted away with it at a pace which caused the Americans (who prided themselves on their muscle) to stare after her in blank amazement.

When next seen she was toiling up a steep street, still ahead of the lazy boy, who slowly followed with the lighter load.

. . . The markets seemed entirely in the hands of the women, and lively scenes they presented to unaccustomed eyes, especially the pig market, held every week, in the square before Madame C's house. At dawn the squealing began, and was kept up till sunset. The carts came in from all the neighboring hamlets, with tubs full of infant pigs, over which the women watched with maternal care till they were safely deposited among the rows of tubs that stood along the walk . . .

If the bargain was struck, they slapped their hands together in a peculiar way, and the new owner clapped her purchase into a meal bag, slung it over her shoulder, and departed with her squirming, squealing treasure as calmly as a Boston lady with a satchel full of ribbons and gloves.

. . . It took two deliberate men nearly a week to split the gnarled logs, and one brisk woman carried them into the cellar and piled them neatly. The men stopped about once an hour to smoke, drink cider, or rest. The woman worked steadily from morning till night, only pausing at noon for a bit of bread and the soup good Coste sent out to her. The men got two francs a day, the woman half a franc; and as nothing was taken out of it for wine or tobacco, her ten cents probably went further than their forty.

. . . No complaint did one hear from these hard working, happy women. The same brave spirit seems to possess them now as that which carried them heroically to their fate in the Revolution, when hundreds of mothers and children were shot at Nantes and died without a murmur.

A long drought parched France that year, and even fertile Brittany suffered. More than once processions of women, led by priests, poured through the gates to go to the Croix du Saint Esprit and pray for rain.

'Why don't the men go also?' Miss Livy asked.

'Ah! They pray to the Virgin, and she listens best to women,' was the answer.

– *from* The Flood in Rome *and* Visit from a King –
(1871)

I t poured steadily for two months, with occasional
flurries of snow, also thunder, likewise hurricanes,
the *tramontàna*, the sirocco, and all the other charming
features of an Italian winter. That nothing might be
wanting, a nice little inundation was got up for their
benefit, December 28th.

Sitting peacefully at breakfast on the morning of
that day, in their cosy apartment, with a fire of cones
and olive wood cheerily burning on the hearth, Jok-
erella, the big cat, purring on the rug, the little coffee pot proudly perched among bread and butter, eggs
and fruit, while the ladies, in dressing gowns and slippers, lounged luxuriously in armchairs, one red, one
blue, one yellow; they (the ladies, not the chairs) were
started by Agrippina, the maid, who burst into the
room like a bomb-shell, announcing, all in one breath,
that the Tiber had risen, inundated the whole city, and
instant death was to be the doom of all.

. . . they hurried forth to see what Father Tiber was
up to. A most reprehensible prank, apparently, for the
lower parts of the city were under water, and many of
the great streets already as full of boats as Venice.

The Corso was a deep and rapid stream, and the

shopkeepers were disconsolately paddling about, trying to rescue their property.

'Our dresses, our beautiful new dresses, where are they now!' wailed the girls, surveying Mazzoni's grand store, with water up to the balcony, where many milliners wrung their hands, lamenting.

The Piazza del Popolo was a lake, with the four stone lions just visible, and still spouting water, though it was a drug in the market. In at the open gate rolled a muddy stream, bearing haystacks, brushwood, and drowned animals along the Corso. People stood on their balconies wondering what they should do, many breakfastless; for how could the *trattoria* boys safely waft their coffee pots across such canals of water? Carriages splashed about in shallower parts with agitated loads, hurrying to drier quarters; many were coming down ladders into boats, and crowds stood waiting their turn with bundles of valuables in their hands.

. . . The soldiers were out in full force, working gallantly to save life and property; making rafts, carrying people on their backs, and going through the inundated streets with boat loads of food for the hungry, shut up in their ill-provided houses. Usually at such times the priests did this work; but now they stood idly looking on, and saying it was a judgment on the people for their treatment of the Pope.

In the Ghetto the disaster was truly terrible, for the flood came so suddenly that the whole quarter was under water in an hour. The scene was pitiful; for here the Jews live packed like sardines in a box, and being washed out with no warning, were utterly destitute. In one street a man and woman were seen wading up to their waists in water, pushing an old mattress before them, on which were three little children, all they had saved.

Later in the day, as boats of provisions came along, women and children swarmed at the windows, crying: 'Bread! bread!' and their wants could not be supplied in spite of the care of the city authorities . . . One poor man, in trying to save a sick wife and his little ones in a cart, upset them, and the babies were drowned at their own door.

. . . Outside the city, houses were carried off, people lost, and bridges swept away, so sudden and violent was the flood. The heavy rains and warm winds melted the snow on the mountains, and swelled the river till it rose higher than at any time since 1805.

Next day the water began to abate, and people made up their minds that the end of the world was not yet. Gentlemen paid visits on the backs of stout soldiers, ladies went shopping in boats, and family dinners were handed in at two-story windows without causing any remark, so quickly do people adapt themselves to the inevitable.

Hardly had the watery excitement subsided when a new event set the city in an uproar.

The King was not expected till the tenth of January; but the kind soul could not wait, and, as soon as the road was passable, he came with 300,000 francs in his hands to see what he could do for his poor Romans. He arrived at 4 a.m., and though unexpected, the news flew through the city, and a crowd turned out with torches to escort him to the Quirinal . . .

For one mortal hour our ladies stood in a pelting rain, and then retired, feeling that the sacrifice of their best hats was all that could reasonably be expected of free-born Americans. They consoled themselves by putting out Pina's fine Italian banner (made in secret, and kept ready for her King, for the *padrona* was *papalino*), and supporting it by two little American flags, the stars and stripes of which much perplexed the boys and donkeys disporting themselves in the Piazza Barberini.

. . . He (the King) was in citizen's dress, and looked like a stout, brown, soldierly man, not so ugly as the pictures of him, but not an Apollo by any means.

Hating ceremony and splendour, he would not have the fine apartments prepared for him, but chose a plain room, saying: 'Keep the finery for my son, if you like; I prefer this.'

He drove through the Ghetto, and all the desolated parts of the city, to see with his own eyes the ruin made; and then desired the city fathers to give to the poor the money they had set apart to make a splendid welcome for him.

He only spent one day, and returned to Florence at night. All Rome was at the station to see him off: ladies with carriages full of flowers, troops of soldiers, and throngs of poor people blessing him like a saint; for this kingly sympathy of his had won all hearts.

– My Boys –

(*from* Aunt Jo's Scrap Bag, 1872)

I like boys and oysters raw; so, though good manners are always pleasing, I don't mind the rough outside burr which repels most people, and perhaps that is the reason why the burrs open and let me see the soft lining and taste the sweet nut hidden inside.

My first well-beloved boy was a certain Frank, to whom I clung at the age of seven with a devotion which I fear he did not appreciate. There were six girls in the house, but I would have nothing to say to them, preferring to tag after Frank, and perfectly happy when he allowed me to play with him. I regret to say that the small youth was something of a tyrant, and one of his favorite amusements was trying to make me cry by slapping my hands with books, hoop-sticks, shoes, anything that came along capable of giving a good stinging blow. I believe I endured these marks of friendship with the fortitude of a young Indian, and felt fully repaid for a blistered palm by hearing Frank tell the other boys, 'She's a brave little thing, and you can't make her cry.'

My chief joy was in romping with him in the long galleries of a piano manufactory behind our house.

What bliss it was to mount one of the cars on which the workmen rolled heavy loads from room to room, and to go thundering down the inclined plains, regardless of the crash that usually awaited us at the bottom! If I could have played football on the Common with my Frank and Billy Babcock, life could have offered me no greater joy at that period. As the prejudices of society forbid this sport, I revenged myself by driving hoop all around the mall without stopping, which the boys could *not* do.

I can remember certain happy evenings, when we snuggled in sofa corners and planned tricks and ate stolen goodies, and sometimes Frank would put his curly head in my lap and let me stroke it when he was tired. What the girls did I don't recollect; their domestic plays were not to my taste, and the only figure that stands out from the dimness of the past is that jolly boy with a twinkling eye . . .

At the mature age of ten, I left home for my first visit to a family of gay and kindly people in – well why not say right out? – Providence. There were no children, and at first I did not mind this, as everyone petted me, especially one of the young men named Christopher. So kind and patient, yet so merry was this good Christy that I took him for my private and particular boy, and loved him dearly; for he got me out of innumerable scrapes, and never was tired of amusing the restless little girl who kept the family in a fever of anxiety by her pranks. *He* never laughed at her mishaps and mistakes, never played tricks upon her like a certain William, who composed the most trying nicknames, and wickedly goaded the wild visitor into all manner of naughtiness.

Christy stood up for her through everything; let her ride the cows, feed the pigs, bang on the piano, and race all over the spice mill, feasting on cinnamon and cloves; brought her down from housetops and fished her out of brooks; never scolded, and never seemed tired of the troublesome friendship of little Torment.

In a week I had exhausted every amusement and was desperately homesick. It has always been my opinion that I should have been speedily restored to the bosom of my family but for Christy, and but for him I should assuredly have run away before the second week was out. He kept me, and in the hour of my disgrace stood by me like a man and a brother.

One afternoon, inspired by a spirit of benevolence, enthusiastic but short-sighted, I collected several poor children in the barn, and regaled them on cake and figs, helping myself freely to the treasures of the pantry without asking leave, meaning to explain afterward. Being discovered before the supplies were entirely exhausted, the patience of the long-suffering matron gave out, and I was ordered up to the garret to reflect upon my sins, and the pleasing prospect of being sent home with the character of the worst child ever known.

My sufferings were deep as I sat upon a fuzzy little trunk all alone in the dull garret, thinking how hard it was to do right, and wondering why I was scolded for feeding the poor when we were expressly bidden to do so. I felt myself an outcast, and bewailed the disgrace I had brought upon my family. Nobody could possibly love such a bad child; and if the mice were to come and eat me then and there – à la Bishop Hatto – it would only be a relief to my friends. At this dark moment I heard Christy say below: 'She meant it kindly, so I wouldn't mind, Fanny,' and then up came my boy full of sympathy and comfort. Seeing the tragic expression of my face, he said not a word, but, sitting down in an old chair, took me on his knee and held me close and quietly, letting the action speak for itself. It did most eloquently; for the kind arm seemed to take me back from that dreadful exile, and the friendly face to assure me without words that I had not sinned beyond forgiveness.

I had not shed a tear before, but now I cried tempestuously, and clung to him like a shipwrecked little mariner in a storm. Neither spoke, but he held me fast and let me cry myself to sleep; for, when the shower was over, a pensive peace fell upon me, and the dim old garret seemed not a prison, but a haven of refuge, since my boy came to share it with me. How long I slept I don't know, but it must have been an hour, at least; yet my good Christy never stirred, only waited patiently till I woke up in the twilight, and was not afraid because he was there. He took me down as meek as a mouse, and kept me by him all that trying evening, screening me from jokes, rebukes, and sober looks; and when I went to bed he came up to kiss me, and to assure me that this awful circumstance should not be reported at home. This took a load off my heart, and I remember fervently thanking him, and telling him I never would forget it.

I never have, though he died long ago, and others have probably forgotten all about the naughty prank . . .

Cy was a comrade after my own heart, and for a summer or two we kept the neighborhood in a ferment by our adventures and hair-breadth escapes. I think I never knew a boy so full of mischief, and my opportunities of judging have been manifold. He did not get into scrapes himself, but possessed a splendid talent for deluding others into them, and then morally remarking: 'There, I told you so!' His way of saying: 'You dars'nt do this or that' was like fire to powder; and why I still live in the possession of all my limbs and senses is a miracle to those who know my youthful friendship with Cy. It was he who incited me to jump off of the highest beam in the barn, to be borne home on a board with a pair of sprained ankles. It was he who dared me to rub my eyes with red peppers, and then sympathisingly led me home blind and roaring with pain. It was he who solemnly assured me that all the little pigs would die in agony if their tails were not cut off, and won me to hold thirteen little squealers while the operation was performed. Those thirteen innocent pink tails haunt me yet, and the memory of that deed has given me a truly Jewish aversion to pork.

I did not know him long, but he was a kindred soul, and must have a place in my list of boys. He is a big, brown man now, and, having done his part in the war, is at work on his farm. We meet sometimes, and though we try to be dignified and proper, it is quite impossible; there is a sly twinkle in Cy's eye that upsets my gravity, and we always burst out laughing at the memory of our early frolics.

My Augustus! Oh, my Augustus! My first little lover, and the most romantic of my boys. At fifteen I met this charming youth, and thought I had found my fate . . .

I fear it was not a very ardent flame, however, for Gus did not write every week, and I did not care a bit; nevertheless, I kept his picture and gave it a sentimental sigh when I happened to think of it, while he sent messages now and then, and devoted himself to his studies like an ambitious boy as he was. I hardly expected to see him again, but soon after the year was out, to my great surprise, he called. I was so fluttered by the appearance of his card that I rather lost my head, and did such a silly thing that it makes me laugh even now. He liked chestnut hair, and, pulling out my combs, I rushed down, theatrically disheveled, hoping to impress my lover with my ardor and my charms.

I expected to find little Gus; but, to my great confusion, a tall being with a beaver in his hand rose to meet me, looking so big and handsome and generally imposing that I could not recover myself for several minutes, and mentally wailed for my combs, feeling like an untidy simpleton.

I don't know whether he thought me a little cracked or not, but he was very friendly and pleasant, and told me his plans, and hoped I would make another visit, and smoothed his beaver, and let me see his tailcoat, and behaved himself like a dear, conceited, clever boy. He did not allude to our love passages, being shy, and I blessed him for it; for really, I don't know what rash thing I might have done under the exciting circumstances. Just as he was going, however, he forgot his cherished hat for a minute, put out both hands, and said heartily, with his old boyish laugh: 'Now you will come, and we'll go boating and berrying, and all the rest of it again, won't we?'

The blue eyes were full of fun and feeling, too, I fancied, as I blushingly retired behind my locks and gave the promise. But I never went, and never saw my little lover any more, for in a few weeks he was dead of a fever, brought on by too much study: and so ended the sad history of my fourth boy.

After this, for many years, I was a boyless being; but . . . the best and dearest of all my flock was my Polish boy, Ladislas Wisniewski – two hiccoughs and a sneeze will give you the name perfectly. Six years ago, as I went down to my early breakfast at our Pension in Vevey, I saw that a stranger had arrived. He was a tall youth, of eighteen or twenty, with a thin,

intelligent face, and the charmingly polite manners of
a foreigner. As the other boarders came in, one by one,
they left the door open, and a draught of cold autumn
air blew in from the stone corridor, making the newcomer cough, shiver, and cast wistful glances towards
the warm corner by the stove. My place was there, and
the heat often oppressed me, so I was glad of an opportunity to move.

A word to Madame Vodoz effected the change;
and at dinner I was rewarded by a grateful smile from
the poor fellow, as he nestled into his warm seat, after
a pause of surprise and a flush of pleasure at the small
kindness from a stranger. We were too far apart to talk
much, but, as he filled his glass, the Pole bowed to me,
and said low in French: 'I drink the good health to
Mademoiselle.'

I returned the wish, but he shook his head with a
sudden shadow on his face, as if the words meant more
than mere compliment to him.

'That boy is sick and needs care. I must see to him,'
said I to myself, as I met him in the afternoon, and
observed the military look of his blue and white suit,
as he touched his cap and smiled pleasantly. I have a
weakness for brave boys in blue, and having discovered that he had been in the late Polish Revolution, my
heart warmed to him at once.

That evening he came to me in the salon, and expressed his thanks in the prettiest broken English I
ever heard. So simple, frank, and grateful was he that a

— *My Boys* —

few words of interest won his little story from him, and
in half an hour we were friends . . .

He told me about the massacre, when five hundred
Poles were shot down by Cossacks in the marketplace,
merely because they sung their national hymn.

'Play me that forbidden air,' I said, wishing to
judge of his skill, for I had heard him practising softly
in the afternoon.

He rose willingly, then glanced about the room
and gave a little shrug which made me ask what he
wanted.

'I look to see if the Baron is here. He is Russian,
and to him my national air will not be pleasing.'

'Then play it. He dare not forbid it here, and I
should rather enjoy that little insult to your bitter enemy,' said I, feeling very indignant with everything
Russian just then.

'Ah, mademoiselle, it is true we are enemies, but
we are also gentlemen,' returned the boy, proving
that *he* at least was one.

. . . Lake Leman will never seem so lovely again
as when Laddie and I roamed about its shores, floated
on its bosom, or laid splendid plans for the future in
the sunny garden of the old chateau. I tried it again
last year, but the charm was gone, for I missed my boy
with his fun, his music, and the frank, fresh affection
he gave his 'little mamma', as he insisted on calling the
lofty spinster who loved him like half-a-dozen grand-
mothers rolled into one.

December roses blossomed in the gardens then, and Laddie never failed to have a posy ready for me at dinner. Few evenings passed without 'confidences' in my corner of the salon, and I still have a pile of merry little notes which I used to find tucked under my door. He called them chapters of a great history we were to write together, and being a '*polisson*' he illustrated it with droll pictures, and a funny mixture of French and English romance . . .

It was not all fun with my boy, however; he had his troubles, and in spite of his cheerfulness he knew what heartache was. Walking in the quaint garden of the Luxembourg one day, he confided to me the little romance of his life. A very touching little romance as he told it, with eloquent eyes and voice and frequent pauses for breath. I cannot give his words, but the simple facts were these: he had grown up with a pretty cousin, and at eighteen was desperately in love with her. She returned his affection, but they could not be happy, for her father wished her to marry a richer man. In Poland, to marry without the consent of parents is to incur lasting disgrace; so Leonore obeyed, and the young pair parted. This had been a heavy sorrow to Laddie, and he rushed into the war, hoping to end his trouble.

'Do you ever hear from your cousin?' I asked, as he walked beside me, looking sadly down the green aisles where kings and queens had loved and parted years ago.

'I only know that she suffers still, for she remembers. Her husband submits to the Russians, and I despise him as I have no English to tell,' and he clenched his hands with the flash of the eye and sudden kindling of the whole face that made him handsome.

He showed me a faded little picture, and when I tried to comfort him, he laid his head down on the pedestal of one of the marble queens who guard the walk, as if he never cared to lift it up again.

But he was all right in a minute, and bravely put away his sorrow with the little picture. He never spoke of it again, and I saw no more shadows on his face till we came to say goodbye.

'You have been so kind to me, I wish I had something beautiful to give you, Laddie,' I said, feeling that it would be hard to get on without my boy.

'This time it is for always; so, as a parting souvenir, give to me the sweet English goodbye.'

As he said this, with a despairing sort of look, as if he could not spare even so humble a friend as myself, my heart was quite rent within me, and, regardless of several prim English ladies, I drew down his tall head and kissed him tenderly, feeling that in this world there were no more meetings for us. Then I ran away and buried myself in an empty railway carriage, hugging the little cologne bottle he had given me.

A year ago he sent me his photograph and a few lines. I acknowledged the receipt of it, but since then not a word has come, and I begin to fear that my boy is dead. Others have appeared to take his place, but they don't suit, and I keep his corner always ready for him if he lives. If he is dead, I am glad to have known so sweet and brave a character, for it does one good to see even as shortlived and obscure a hero as my Polish boy, whose dead December rose embalms for me the memory of Varjo, the last and dearest of my boys.

– *from* Happy Women –
(1868)

O ne of the trials of womankind is the fear of being an old maid. To escape this dreadful doom,
young girls rush into matrimony with a recklessness
which astonishes the beholder; never pausing to remember that the loss of liberty, happiness, and self
respect is poorly repaid by the barren honor of being
called 'Mrs' instead of 'Miss'.

. . . Here is L., a rich man's daughter; pretty, accomplished, sensible, and good. She tried fashionable
life and found that it did not satisfy her. No lover was
happy enough to make a response in her heart, and
at twenty-three she looked about her for something to
occupy and interest her. She was attracted toward the
study of medicine; became absorbed in it; went alone
to Paris and London; studied faithfully; received her
diploma, and, having practiced successfully for a time,
was appointed the resident physician of a city hospital . . . she finds no time for ennui, unhappiness, or
the vague longing for something to fill heart and life,
which leads so many women to take refuge in frivolous
or dangerous pursuits and interests. She never talks of
her mission or her rights, but beautifully fulfils the one
and quietly assumes the other . . .

M. . . . Poor, yet attractive, through natural gifts and graces, to her came the great temptation of such a girl's life – a rich lover; an excellent young man, but her inferior in all respects. She felt this, and so did he, but hoping that love would make them equals, he urged his suit.

'If I loved him,' she said, 'my way would be plain, and I should not hesitate a minute. But I do not; I've tried . . . People tell me that I am foolish to reject this good fortune; that it is my duty to accept it; that I shall get on very well without love, and talk as if it were a business transaction. It is hard to say 'No'; but . . . in marriage I want to look up, not down. I cannot make it seem right to take this offer, and I must let it go, for I dare not sell my liberty.'

. . . S. is poor, plain, ungifted, and ordinary in all things but one – a cheerful, helpful spirit, that loves its neighbors better than itself, and cannot rest till it has proved its sincerity. Few, so placed, would have lived forty hard, dull years without becoming either sharp and sour, or bitter and blue, but S. is as sweet and sunny as a child . . . Finding her round of home duties too small for her benevolence, she became one of the home missionaries, whose reports are never read, whose salaries are never paid of earth. Poverty-stricken homes, sick beds, sinful souls, and sorrowing hearts attract her as irresistibly as pleasure attracts other women, and she faithfully ministers to such, unknown and unrewarded.

'I never had a lover, and I never can have you know. I'm *so* plain,' she says, with a smile that is pathetic in its humility, its unconscious wistfulness.

She is mistaken here; for there are many to whom that plain face is beautiful, that helpful hand very dear. Her lovers are not of the romantic sort, but old women, little children, erring men and forlorn girls . . .

A. is a woman who in the course of an unusually varied experience has seen so much of what a wise man has called 'the tragedy of modern married life', that she is afraid to try it. Knowing that for one of a peculiar nature like herself such an experiment would be doubly hazardous, she has obeyed instinct and become a chronic old maid. Filial and fraternal love must satisfy her, and grateful that such ties are possible, she lives for them and is content. Literature is a fond and faithful spouse, and the little family that has sprung up around her, though perhaps unlovely and uninteresting to others, is a profitable source of satisfaction to her maternal heart. After a somewhat tempestuous voyage, she is glad to find herself in a quiet haven . . .

My sisters, don't be afraid of the words, 'old maid', for it is in your power to make this a term of honor, not reproach. It is not necessary to be a sour, spiteful spinster, with nothing to do but brew tea, talk scandal and tend a pocket handkerchief. No, the world is full of work, needing all the heads, hearts, and hands we can bring to do it. Never was there so splendid an opportunity for women to enjoy their liberty and prove that they deserve it by using it wisely. If love comes as it should come, accept it in God's name and be worthy of His best blessing. If it never comes, then in God's name reject the shadow of it, for that can never satisfy a hungry heart. Do not be ashamed to own the truth – do not be daunted by the fear of ridicule and loneliness, nor saddened by the loss . . . Be true to yourselves; cherish whatever talent you possess, and in using it faithfully for the good of others, you will most assuredly find happiness for yourself, and make of life no failure, but a beautiful success.

– Hospital Sketches –
(1863)

Chapter One: Obtaining Supplies

'I want something to do.'

This remark being addressed to the world in general, no one in particular felt it their duty to reply; so I repeated it to the smaller world about me, received the following suggestions, and settled the matter by answering my own inquiry, as people are apt to do when very much in earnest.

'Write a book,' quoth the author of my being.

'Don't know enough, sir. First live, then write.'

'Try teaching again,' suggested my mother.

'No thank you, ma'am, ten years of that is enough.'

'Take a husband like my Darby, and fulfill your mission,' said sister Joan, home on a visit.

'Can't afford expensive luxuries, Mrs Coobiddy.'

'Turn actress, and immortalize your name,' said sister Vashti, striking an attitude.

'I won't.'

'Go nurse the soldiers,' said my young brother, Tom, panting for 'the tented field'.

'I will!'

So far, very good. Here was the will – now for the

way. At first sight not a foot of it appeared, but that didn't matter, for the Periwinkles are a hopeful race; their crest is an anchor, with three cock-a-doodles crowing atop. They all wear rose-colored spectacles, and are lineal descendants of the inventor of aerial architecture. An hour's conversation on the subject set the whole family in a blaze of enthusiasm. A model hospital was erected, and each member had accepted an honorable post therein. The paternal P. was chaplain, the maternal P. was matron, and all the youthful P.'s filled the pod of futurity with achievements whose brilliancy eclipsed the glories of the present and the past. Arriving at this satisfactory conclusion, the meeting adjourned, and the fact that Miss Tribulation was available as army nurse went abroad on the wings of the wind.

In a few days a townswoman heard of my desire, approved of it, and brought about an interview with one of the sisterhood which I wished to join, who was at home on a furlough, and able and willing to satisfy all inquiries. A morning chat with Miss General S. – we hear no end of Mrs Generals, why not a Miss? – produced three results: I felt that I could do the work, was offered a place, and accepted it, promising not to desert, but stand ready to march on Washington at an hour's notice.

A few days were necessary for the letter containing my request and recommendation to reach headquarters, and another, containing my commission, to return; therefore no time was to be lost; and heartily thanking my pair of friends, I tore home through the December slush as if the rebels were after me, and like many another recruit, burst in upon my family with the announcement: 'I've enlisted!'

An impressive silence followed. Tom, the irrepressible, broke it with a slap on the shoulder and the graceful compliment: 'Old Trib, you're a trump!'

'Thank you; then I'll take something,' which I did, in the shape of dinner, reeling off my news at the rate of three dozen words to a mouthful; and as everyone else talked equally fast, and all together, the scene was most inspiring.

As boys going to sea immediately become nautical in speech, walk as if they already had their 'sea legs' on, and shiver their timbers on all possible occasions, so I turned military at once, called my dinner my rations, saluted all new comers, and ordered a dress parade that very afternoon. Having reviewed every rag I possessed, I detailed some for picket duty while airing over the fence; some to the sanitary influences of the wash tub; others to mount guard in the trunk; while the weak and wounded went to the work basket Hospital, to be made ready for active service again. To this squad I devoted myself for a week; but all was done, and I had time to get powerfully impatient before the letter came. It did arrive however, and brought a disappointment along with its good will and friendliness, for it told me that the place in the Armory Hospital that I supposed I was to take, was already filled, and a much less desirable one at Hurly-burly House was offered instead.

'That's just your luck, Trib. I'll tote your trunk up garret for you again; for of course you won't go,' Tom remarked, with the disdainful pity which small boys affect when they get into their teens.

I was wavering in my secret soul, but that settled the matter, and I crushed him on the spot with martial brevity: 'It is now one; I shall march at six.'

I have a confused recollection of spending the afternoon in pervading the house like an executive whirlwind, with my family swarming after me, all working, talking, prophesying and lamenting, while I packed my 'go-abroady' possessions, tumbled the rest into two big boxes, danced on the lids till they shut, and gave them in charge, with the direction: 'If I never come back, make a bonfire of them.'

Then I choked down a cup of tea, generously salted instead of sugared, by some agitated relative, shouldered my knapsack – it was only a traveling bag, but do let me preserve the unities – hugged my family three times all round without a vestige of unmanly emotion, till a certain dear old lady broke down upon my neck, with a despairing sort of wail: 'Oh, my dear, my dear, how can I let you go?'

'I'll stay if you say so, mother.'

'But I don't; go, and the Lord will take care of you.'

Much of the Roman matron's courage had gone

into the Yankee matron's composition, and, in spite of her tears, she would have sent ten sons to the war, had she possessed them, as freely as she sent one daughter, smiling and flapping on the doorstep till I vanished, though the eyes that followed me were very dim, and the handkerchief she waved was very wet.

My transit from The Gables to the village depot was a funny mixture of good wishes and goodbyes, mud puddles and shopping. A December twilight is not the most cheering time to enter upon a somewhat perilous enterprise, and, but for the presence of Vashti and neighbor Thorn, I fear that I might have added a drop of the briny to the native moisture of: 'The town I left behind me,' though I'd no thought of giving out: oh, bless you, no! When the engine screeched: 'Here we are,' I clutched my escort in a fervent embrace, and skipped into the car with as blithe a farewell as if going on a bridal tour – though I believe brides don't usually wear cavernous black bonnets and fuzzy brown coats, with a hairbrush, a pair of rubbers, two books, and a bag of gingerbread distorting the pockets of the same. If I thought that anyone would believe it, I'd boldly state that I slept from C. to B., which would simplify matters immensely; but as I know they wouldn't, I'll confess that the head under the funereal coal-hod fermented with all manner of high thoughts and heroic purposes 'to do or die': perhaps both; and the heart under the fuzzy brown coat felt very tender with the memory of the dear old lady, probably sobbing over her army socks and the loss of her topsy-turvy Trib. At this juncture I took the veil, and what I did behind it is nobody's business; but I maintain that the soldier who cries when his mother says 'Goodbye', is the boy to fight best, and die bravest, when the time comes, or go back to her better than he went.

Till nine o'clock I trotted about the city streets, doing those last errands which no woman would even go to heaven without attempting, if she could. Then I went to my usual refuge, and, fully intending to keep awake, as a sort of vigil appropriate to the occasion, fell fast asleep and dreamed propitious dreams till my rosy-faced cousin waked me with a kiss.

A bright day smiled upon my enterprise, and at ten I reported myself to my General, received last instructions and no end of the sympathetic encouragement which women give, in look, touch, and tone more effectually than in words. The next step was to get a free pass to Washington, for I'd no desire to waste my substance on railroad companies when 'the boys' needed even a spinster's mite. A friend of mine had procured such a pass, and I was bent on doing likewise, though I had to face the president of the railroad to accomplish it. I'm a bashful individual, though I can't get anyone to believe it; so it cost me a great effort to poke about the Worcester depot till the right door appeared, then walk into a room containing several gentlemen, and blunder out my request in a high state of stammer and blush. Nothing could have been more courteous than this dreaded President, but it was evident that I had made as absurd a demand as if I had asked for the nose off his respectable face. He referred me to the Governor at the State House, and I backed out, leaving him no doubt to regret that such mild maniacs were left at large. Here was a Scylla and Charybdis business: as if a President wasn't trying enough, without the Governor of Massachusetts and the hub of the hub piled on top of that.

'I never can do it,' thought I.

'Tom will hoot at you if you don't,' whispered the inconvenient little voice that is always goading people to the performance of disagreeable duties, and always appeals to the most effective agent to produce the proper result. The idea of allowing any boy that ever wore a felt basin and a shoddy jacket with a microscopic tail, to crow over me, was preposterous, so giving myself a mental slap for such faint-heartedness, I streamed away across the Common, wondering if I ought to say: 'your Honor', or simply 'Sir', and decided upon the latter, fortifying myself with recollections of an evening in a charming green library, where I beheld the Governor placidly consuming oysters, and laughing as if Massachusetts was a myth, and he had no heavier burden on his shoulders than his host's handsome hands.

Like an energetic fly in a very large cobweb, I struggled through the State House, getting into all the wrong rooms and none of the right, till I turned desperate, and went into one, resolving not to come

out till I'd made somebody hear and answer me. I suspect that of all the wrong places I had blundered into,
this was the most so. But I didn't care; and, though the
apartment was full of soldiers, surgeons, starers, and
spittoons, I cornered a perfectly incapable person, and
proceeded to pump for information with the following
result: 'Was the Governor anywhere about?'

No, he wasn't.

'Could he tell me where to look?'

No, he couldn't.

'Did he know anything about free passes?'

No, he didn't.

'Was there anyone there of whom I could inquire?'

Not a person.

'Did he know of any place where information
could be obtained?'

Not a place.

'Could he throw the smallest gleam of light upon
the matter, in any way?'

Not a ray.

I am naturally irascible, and if I could have shaken
this negative gentleman vigorously, the relief would
have been immense. The prejudices of society forbidding this mode of redress, I merely glowered at him;
and, before my wrath found vent in words, my General
appeared, having seen me from an opposite window,
and come to know what I was about. At her command
the languid gentleman woke up, and troubled himself
to remember that Major or Sergeant or something Mc

K. knew all about the tickets, and his office was in Milk Street. I perked up instanter, and then, as if the exertion was too much for him, what did this animated wet blanket do but add: 'I think Mc K. may have left Milk Street, now, and I don't know where he has gone.'

'Never mind; the newcomers will know where he has moved to, my dear, so don't be discouraged; and if you don't succeed, come to me, and we will see what to do next,' said my General.

I blessed her in a fervent manner and a cool hall, fluttered round the corner, and bore down upon Milk Street, bent on discovering Mc K. if such a being was to be found. He wasn't, and the ignorance of the neighborhood was really pitiable. Nobody knew anything, and after tumbling over bundles of leather, bumping against big boxes, being nearly annihilated by descending bales, and sworn at by aggravated truckmen, I finally elicited the advice to look for Mc K. in Haymarket Square. Who my informant was I've really forgotten; for, having hailed several busy gentlemen, some one of them fabricated this delusive quietus for the perturbed spirit, who instantly departed to the sequestered locality he named. If I had been in search of the Koh-i-noor diamond I should have been as likely to find it there as any vestige of Mc K. I stared at signs, inquired in shops, invaded an eating house, visited the recruiting tent in the middle of the Square, made myself a nuisance generally, and accumulated mud enough to retard another Nile. All in vain: and

I mournfully turned my face toward the General's, feeling that I should be forced to enrich the railroad company after all; when, suddenly, I beheld that admirable young man, brother-in-law Darby Coobiddy, Esq. I arrested him with a burst of news, and wants, and woes, which caused his manly countenance to lose its usual repose.

'Oh, my dear boy, I'm going to Washington at five, and I can't find the free ticket man, and there won't be time to see Joan, and I'm so tired and cross I don't know what to do; and will you help me, like a cherub as you are?'

'Oh, yes, of course. I know a fellow who will set us right,' responded Darby, mildly excited, and darting into some kind of an office, held counsel with an invisible angel, who sent him out radiant. 'All serene. I've got him. I'll see you through the business, and then get Joan from the Dove Cote in time to see you off.'

I'm a woman's rights woman, and if any man had offered help in the morning, I should have condescendingly refused it, sure that I could do everything as well, if not better, myself. My strong mindedness had rather abated since then, and I was now quite ready to be a 'timid trembler', if necessary. Dear me! How easily Darby did it all: he just asked one question, received an answer, tucked me under his arm, and in ten minutes I stood in the presence of Mc K., the Desired.

'Now my troubles are over,' thought I, and as usual was direfully mistaken.

'You will have to get a pass from Dr H., in Temple Place, before I can give you a pass, madam,' answered Mc K., as blandly as if he wasn't carrying desolation to my soul.

Oh, indeed! Why didn't he send me to Dorchester Heights, India Wharf, or Bunker Hill Monument, and be done with it? Here I was, after a morning's tramp, down in some place about Dock Square, and was told to step to Temple Place. Nor was that all; he might as well have asked me to catch a hummingbird, toast a salamander, or call on the man in the moon, as find a Doctor at home at the busiest hour of the day. It was a blow; but weariness had extinguished enthusiasm, and resignation clothed me as a garment. I sent Darby for Joan, and doggedly paddled off, feeling that mud was my nativement, and quite sure that the evening papers would announce the appearance of the Wandering Jew, in feminine habiliments.

'Is Dr H. in?'

'No, mum, he aint.'

Of course he wasn't; I knew that before I asked: and, considering it all in the light of a hollow mockery, added, 'When will he probably return?'

If the damsel had said: 'ten tonight,' I should have felt a grim satisfaction, in the fulfillment of my own dark prophecy; but she said: 'At two, mum;' and I felt it a personal insult.

'I'll call, then. Tell him my business is important,' with which mysteriously delivered message I departed, hoping that I left her consumed with curiosity; for mud rendered me an object of interest.

By way of resting myself, I crossed the Common, for the third time, bespoke the carriage, got some lunch, packed my purchases, smoothed my plumage, and was back again, as the clock struck two. The Doctor hadn't come yet; and I was morally certain that he would not, till, having waited till the last minute, I was driven to buy a ticket, and, five minutes after the irrevocable deed was done, he would be at my service, with all manner of helpful documents and directions. Everything goes by contraries with me; so, having made up my mind to be disappointed, of course I wasn't; for, presently, in walked Dr H., and no sooner had he heard my errand, and glanced at my credentials, than he said, with the most engaging readiness: 'I will give you the order, with pleasure, madam.'

. . . Why I was sent to a steamboat office for car tickets, is not for me to say, though I went as meekly as I should have gone to the Probate Court, if sent. A fat, easy gentleman gave me several bits of paper, with coupons attached, with a warning not to separate them, which instantly inspired me with a yearning to pluck them apart, and see what came of it. But, remembering through what fear and tribulation I had obtained them, I curbed Satan's promptings, and, clutching my prize, as if it were my pass to the Elysian Fields, I hurried home. Dinner was rapidly consumed; Joan enlightened, comforted, and kissed; the dearest of apple-faced cousins hugged; the kindest of apple-faced cousins' fathers subjected to the same process; and I mounted the ambulance, baggage wagon, or anything you please but hack, and drove away, too tired to feel excited, sorry, or glad.

Chapter Two: A Forward Movement

As travelers like to give their own impressions of a journey, though every inch of the way may have been described a half a dozen times before, I add some of the notes made by the way, hoping that they will amuse the reader, and convince the skeptical that such a being as Nurse Periwinkle does exist, that she really did go to Washington, and that these Sketches are not romance.

New York Train: 7 p.m. Spinning along to take the boat at New London. Very comfortable; munch gingerbread, and Mrs C.'s fine pear, which deserves honorable mention, because my first loneliness was comforted by it, and pleasant recollections of both kindly sender and bearer. Look much at Dr H.'s paper of directions: put my tickets in every conceivable place, that they may be get-at-able, and finish by losing them entirely. Suffer agonies till a compassionate neighbor pokes them out of a crack with his penknife. Put them in the inmost corner of my purse, that in the deepest recesses of my pocket, pile a collection of miscellaneous articles atop, and pin up the whole. Just get composed, feeling that I've done my best to keep them safely, when the Conductor appears, and I'm forced to rout them all out again, exposing my precautions, and getting into a flutter at keeping the man waiting. Finally, fasten them on the seat before me, and keep one eye steadily upon the yellow torments, till I forget all about them, in chat with the gentleman who shares my seat. Having heard complaints of the absurd way in which American women become images of petrified propriety, if addressed by strangers, when traveling alone, the inborn perversity of my nature causes me to assume an entirely opposite style of deportment; and, finding my companion hails from Little Athens, is acquainted with several of my three hundred and sixty-five cousins, and in every way a respectable and respectful member of society, I put my bashfulness in my pocket, and plunge into a long conversation on the war, the weather, music, Carlyle, skating, genius, hoops, and the immortality of the soul.

10 p.m. Very sleepy. Nothing to be seen outside, but darkness made visible; nothing inside but every variety of bunch into which the human form can be twisted, rolled, or 'massed', as Miss Prescott says of her jewels. Everyman's legs sprawl drowsily, every woman's head (but mine) nods, till it finally settles on somebody's shoulder, a new proof of the truth of the everlasting oak and vine simile; children fret; lovers whisper; old folks snore, and somebody privately imbibes brandy, when the lamps go out. The penetrat-

ing perfume rouses the multitude, causing some to start up, like war horses at the smell of powder. When the lamps are relighted, everyone laughs, sniffs, and looks inquiringly at his neighbor: everyone but a stout gentleman, who, with well-gloved hands folded upon his broad-cloth rotundity, sleeps onimpressively. Had he been innocent, he would have waked up; for, to slumber in that babe-like manner, with a car full of giggling, staring, sniffing humanity, was simply preposterous. Public suspicion was down upon him at once. I doubt if the appearance of a flat black bottle with a label would have settled the matter more effectually than did the over dignified and profound repose of this short-sighted being. His moral neckcloth, virtuous boots, and pious attitude availed him nothing, and it was well he kept his eyes shut, for 'Humbug!' twinkled at him from every windowpane, brass nail and human eye around him.

11 p.m. In the boat *City of Boston*, escorted thither by my car acquaintance, and deposited in the cabin. Trying to look as if the greater portion of my life had been passed onboard boats, but painfully conscious that I don't know the first thing; so sit bolt upright, and stare about me till I hear one lady say to another: 'We must secure our berths at once,' whereupon I dart at one, and, while leisurely taking off my cloak, wait to discover what the second move may be. Several ladies draw the curtains that hang in a semi-circle before each nest: instantly I whisk mine smartly together, and then

peep out to see what next. Gradually, on hooks above the blue and yellow drapery, appear the coats and bonnets of my neighbors, while their boots and shoes, in every imaginable attitude, assert themselves below, as if their owners had committed suicide in a body. A violent creaking, scrambling, and fussing, causes the fact that people are going regularly to bed to dawn upon my mind. Of course they are; and so am I – but pause at the seventh pin, remembering that, as I was born to be drowned, an eligible opportunity now presents itself; and, having twice escaped a watery grave, the third immersion will certainly extinguish my vital spark. The boat is new, but if it ever intends to blow up, spring a leak, catch afire, or be run into, it will do the deed tonight, because I'm here to fulfill my destiny. With tragic calmness I resign myself, replace my pins, lash my purse and papers together, with my handkerchief, examine the saving circumference of my hoop, and look about me for any means of deliverance when the moist moment shall arrive; for I've no intention of folding my hands and bubbling to death without an energetic splashing first. Barrels, hen coops, portable settees, and life preservers do not adorn the cabin, as they should; and, roving wildly to and fro, my eye sees no ray of hope till it falls upon a plump old lady, devoutly reading in the cabin Bible, and a voluminous nightcap. I remember that, at the swimming school, fat girls always floated best, and in an instant my plan is laid. At the first alarm I firmly attach myself to the plump lady, and cling to her through fire and water; for I feel that my old enemy, the cramp, will seize me by the foot, if I attempt to swim; and, though I can hardly expect to reach Jersey City with myself and my baggage in as good condition as I hoped, I might manage to get picked up by holding to my fat friend; if not it will be a comfort to feel that I've made an effort and shall die in good society. Poor dear woman! How little she dreamed, as she read and rocked, with her cap in a high state of starch, and her feet comfortably cooking at the register, what fell designs were hovering about her, and how intently a small but determined eye watched her, till it suddenly closed.

Sleep got the better of fear to such an extent that my boots appeared to gape, and my bonnet nodded on its peg, before I gave in. Having piled my cloak, bag, rubbers, books and umbrella on the lower shelf, I drowsily swarmed onto the upper one, tumbling down a few times, and excoriating the knobby portions of my frame in the act. A very brief nap on the upper roost was enough to set me gasping as if a dozen feather beds and the whole boat were laid over me. Out I turned; and after a series of convulsions, which caused my neighbor to ask if I wanted the stewardess, I managed to get my luggage up and myself down. But even in the lower berth, my rest was not unbroken, for various articles kept dropping off the little shelf at the bottom of the bed, and every time I flew up, thinking my hour had come, I bumped my head severely against the little shelf at the top, evidently put there for that express purpose. At last, after listening to the swash of the waves outside, wondering if the machinery usually creaked in that way, and watching a knot hole in the side of my berth, sure that death would creep in there as soon as I took my eye from it, I dropped asleep, and dreamed of muffins.

5 a.m. On deck, trying to wake up and enjoy an east wind and a morning fog, and a twilight sort of view of something on the shore. Rapidly achieve my purpose, and do enjoy every moment, as we go rushing through the Sound, with steamboats passing up and down, lights dancing on the shore, mist wreaths slowly furling off, and a pale pink sky above us, as the sun comes up.

7 a.m. In the cars, at Jersey City. Much fuss with tickets, which one man scribbles over, another snips, and a third 'makes note on'. Partake of refreshment, in the gloom of a very large and dirty depot. Think that my sandwiches would be more relishing without so strong a flavor of napkin, and my gingerbread more easy of consumption if it had not been pulverized by being sat upon.

People act as if early traveling didn't agree with them. Children scream and scamper; men smoke and growl; women shiver and fret; porters swear; great truck horses pace up and down with loads of baggage; and everyone seems to get into the wrong car, and come tumbling out again. One man, with three children, a dog, a birdcage, and several bundles, puts himself and his possessions into every possible place where a man, three children, dog, birdcage and bundles could be got, and is satisfied with none of them. I follow their movements, with an interest that is really exhausting, and, as they vanish, hope for rest, but don't get it. A strong-minded woman, with a tumbler in her hand, and no cloak or shawl on, comes rushing through the car, talking loudly to a small porter, who lugs a folding bed after her, and looks as if life were a burden to him.

'You promised to have it ready. It is not ready. It must be a car with a water jar, the windows must be shut, the fire must be kept up, the blinds must be down. No, this won't do. I shall go through the whole train, and suit myself, for you promised to have it ready. It is not ready,' etc., all through again, like a hand organ. She haunted the cars, the depot, the office and baggage room, with her bed, her tumbler, and her tongue, till the train started; and a sense of fervent gratitude filled my soul, when I found that she and her unknown invalid were not to share our car.

Philadelphia. An old place, full of Dutch women, in 'bellus top' bonnets, selling vegetables, in long, open markets. Everyone seems to be scrubbing their white steps. All the houses look like tidy jails, with their outside shutters. Several have crape on the door handles, and many have flags flying from roof or balcony. Few men appear, and the women seem to do the business, which, perhaps, accounts for its being so well done. Pass fine buildings, but don't know what they are. Would like to stop and see my native city; for, having left it at the tender age of two, my recollections are not vivid.

Baltimore. A big, dirty, shippy, shiftless place, full of goats, geese, colored people, and coal, at least the part of it I see. Pass near the spot where the riot took place, and feel as if I should enjoy throwing a stone at somebody, hard. Find a guard at the ferry, the depot, and here and there, along the road. A camp whitens one hillside, and a cavalry training school, or whatever it should be called, is a very interesting sight, with quantities of horses and riders galloping, marching, leaping, and skirmishing, over all manner of break-neck places. A party of English people get in: the men, with sandy hair and red whiskers, all trimmed alike, to a hair; rough gray coats, very rosy, clean faces, and a fine, full way of speaking, which is particularly agreeable, after our slip-shod American gabble. The two ladies wear funny velvet fur-trimmed hoods; are done up, like compact bundles, in tartan shawls; and look as if bent on seeing everything thoroughly. The devotion of one elderly John Bull to his red-nosed spouse was really beautiful to behold. She was plain and cross, and fussy and stupid, but J. B., Esq., read no papers when she was awake, turned no cold shoulder when she wished to sleep, and cheerfully said: 'Yes, me dear,' to every wish or want the wife of his bosom expressed. I quite warmed to the excellent man, and asked a question or two, as the only means of expressing my good will. He answered very civilly, but evidently hadn't been used to being addressed by strange women in public conveyances; and Mrs B. fixed her green eyes upon me, as if she thought me a forward huzzy, or whatever is good English for a presuming young woman. The pair left their friends before we reached Washington; and the last I saw of them was a vision of a large plaid lady, stalking grimly away, on the arm of a rosy, stout gentleman, loaded with rugs, bags, and books, but still devoted, still smiling, and waving a hearty: 'Fare ye well! We'll meet ye at Willard's on Chusday.'

Soon after their departure we had an accident; for no long journey in America would be complete without one. A coupling iron broke; and, after leaving the last car behind us, we waited for it to come up, which it did, with a crash that knocked everyone forward on their faces, and caused several old ladies to screech dismally Hats flew off, bonnets were flattened, the stove skipped, the lamps fell down, the water jar turned a somersault, and the wheel just over which I sat received some damage. Of course, it became necessary for all the men to get out, and stand about in everybody's way, while repairs were made; and for the women to wrestle their heads out of the windows, asking ninety-nine foolish questions to one sensible one. A few wise females seized this favorable moment to better their seats, well knowing that few men can face the wooden stare with which they regard the former possessors of the places they have invaded.

The country through which we passed did not seem so very unlike that which I had left, except that it was more level and less wintry. In summertime the wide fields would have shown me new sights, and the way-side hedges blossomed with new flowers; now, everything was sere and sodden, and a general air of shiftlessness prevailed, which would have caused a New England farmer much disgust, and a strong desire to 'buckle to', and 'right up' things. Dreary little houses, with chimneys built outside, with clay and rough sticks piled crosswise, as we used to build cob towers, stood in barren looking fields, with cow, pig, or mule lounging about the door.

We often passed colored people, looking as if they had come out of a picture book, or off the stage, but not at all the sort of people I'd been accustomed to see at the North. Way-side encampments made the fields and lanes gay with blue coats and the glitter of buttons. Military washes flapped and fluttered on the fences; pots were steaming in the open air; all sorts of tableaux seen through the openings of tents, and everywhere the boys threw up their caps and cut capers as we passed.

Washington. It was dark when we arrived; and, but for the presence of another friendly gentleman, I should have yielded myself a helpless prey to the first overpowering hackman, who insisted that I wanted to go just where I didn't. Putting me into the conveyance I belonged in, my escort added to the obligation by pointing out the objects of interest which we passed in our long drive. Though I'd often been told that Washington was a spacious place, its visible magnitude quite took my breath away, and of course I quoted Randolph's expression: 'A city of magnificent distances,' as I suppose everyone does when they see it. The Capitol was so like the pictures that hang opposite the staring Father of his Country, in boarding houses and hotels, that it did not impress me, except to recall the time when I was sure that Cinderella went to housekeeping in just such a place, after she had married the inflammable Prince; though, even at that early period, I had my doubts as to the wisdom of a match whose foundation was of glass.

The White House was lighted up, and carriages were rolling in and out of the great gate. I stared hard at the famous East Room, and would have liked a peep through the crack of the door. My old gentleman was indefatigable in his attentions, and I said: 'Splendid!' to everything he pointed out, though I suspect I often admired the wrong place, and missed the right.

Pennsylvania Avenue, with its bustle, lights, music, and military, made me feel as if I'd crossed the water and landed somewhere in Carnival time. Coming to less noticeable parts of the city, my companion fell silent, and I meditated upon the perfection which Art had attained in America: having just passed a bronze

statue of some hero, who looked like a black Method-
ist minister, in a cocked hat, above the waist, and a
tipsy squire below; while his horse stood like an opera
dancer, on one leg, in a high, but somewhat remarkable wind, which blew his mane one way and his massive tail the other.

'Hurly-burly House, ma'am!' called a voice, startling me from my reverie, as we stopped before a great
pile of buildings, with a flag flying before it, sentinels
at the door, and a very trying quantity of men lounging
about. My heart beat rather faster than usual, and it
suddenly struck me that I was very far from home; but
I descended with dignity, wondering whether I should
be stopped for want of a countersign, and forced to pass
the night in the street. Marching boldly up the steps,
I found that no form was necessary, for the men fell
back, the guard touched their caps, a boy opened the
door, and, as it closed behind me, I felt that I was fairly
started, and Nurse Periwinkle's Mission was begun.

Chapter Three: A Day

'They've come! They've come! Hurry up, ladies –
you're wanted.'

'Who have come? the rebels?'

This sudden summons in the gray dawn was somewhat startling to a three days' nurse like myself, and,
as the thundering knock came at our door, I sprang up
in my bed, prepared

'To gird my woman's form, And on the ramparts die,' if necessary; but my roommate took it more coolly, and, as she began a rapid toilet, answered my bewildered question,

'Bless you, no child; it's the wounded from Fredericksburg; forty ambulances are at the door, and we shall have our hands full in fifteen minutes.'

'What shall we have to do?'

'Wash, dress, feed, warm and nurse them for the next three months, I dare say. Eighty beds are ready, and we were getting impatient for the men to come. Now you will begin to see hospital life in earnest, for you won't probably find time to sit down all day and may think yourself fortunate if you get to bed by midnight. Come to me in the ballroom when you are ready; the worst cases are always carried there, and I shall need your help.'

So saying, the energetic little woman twirled her hair into a button at the back of her head, in a 'cleared for action' sort of style, and vanished, wrestling her way into a feminine kind of pea jacket as she went.

I am free to confess that I had a realizing sense of the fact that my hospital bed was not a bed of roses just then, or the prospect before me one of unmingled rapture. My three days' experiences had begun with a death, and, owing to the defalcation of another nurse, a somewhat abrupt plunge into the superintendence of a ward containing forty beds, where I spent my shining hours washing faces, serving rations, giving medicine, and sitting in a very hard chair, with pneumonia on one side, diptheria on the other, five typhoids on the opposite, and a dozen dilapidated patriots, hopping, lying, and lounging about, all staring more or less at the new 'nuss', who suffered untold agonies, but concealed them under as matronly an aspect as a spinster could assume, and blundered through her trying labors with a Spartan firmness, which I hope they appreciated, but am afraid they didn't. Having a taste for 'ghastliness', I had rather longed for the wounded to arrive, for rheumatism wasn't heroic, neither was liver complaint, or measles; even fever had lost its charms since 'bathing burning brows' had been used up in romances, real and ideal; but when I peeped into the dusky street lined with what I at first had innocently called market carts, now unloading their sad freight at our door, I recalled sundry reminiscences I had heard from nurses of longer standing, my ardor experienced a sudden chill, and I indulged in a most unpatriotic wish that I was safe at home again, with a quiet day before me, and no necessity for being hustled up, as if I were a hen and had only to hop off my roost, give my plumage a peck, and be ready for action.

A second bang at the door sent this recreant desire to the right about, as a little woolly head popped in, and Joey, (a six years' old contraband), announced: 'Miss Blank is jes' wild fer ye, and says fly round right away. They's comin' in, I tell yer, heaps of 'em – one was took out dead, and I see him: Hi! Warn't he a goner!'

With which cheerful intelligence the imp scuttled away, singing like a blackbird, and I followed, feeling that Richard was not himself again, and wouldn't be for a long time to come.

The first thing I met was a regiment of the vilest odors that ever assaulted the human nose, and took it by storm. Cologne, with its seven and seventy evil savors, was a posy bed to it; and the worst of this affliction was, everyone had assured me that it was a chronic weakness of all hospitals, and I must bear it. I did, armed with lavender water, with which I so besprinkled myself and premises, that, like my friend Sairy, I was soon known among my patients as 'the nurse with the bottle'. Having been run over by three excited surgeons, bumped against by migratory coal-hods, water pails, and small boys, nearly scalded by an avalanche of newly-filled teapots, and hopelessly entangled in a knot of colored sisters coming to wash, I progressed by slow stages upstairs and down, till the main hall was reached, and I paused to take breath and a survey. There they were! 'Our brave boys', as the papers justly call them, for cowards could hardly have been so riddled with shot and shell, so torn and shattered, nor have borne suffering for which we have no name, with an uncomplaining fortitude, which made one glad to cherish each as a brother. In they came, some on stretchers, some in men's arms, some feebly staggering along propped on rude crutches, and one lay stark and still with covered face, as a comrade gave his name to be recorded before they carried him away to the dead house. All was hurry and confusion; the hall was full of these wrecks of humanity, for the most exhausted could not reach a bed till duly ticketed and registered; the walls were lined with rows of such as could sit, the floor covered with the more disabled, the steps and doorways filled with helpers and lookers-on; the sound of many feet and voices made that usually quiet hour as noisy as noon; and, in the midst of it all, the matron's motherly face brought more comfort to many a poor soul, than the cordial draughts she administered, or the cheery words that welcomed all, making of the hospital a home.

The sight of several stretchers, each with its legless, armless, or desperately wounded occupant, entering my ward, admonished me that I was there to work, not to wonder or weep; so I corked up my feelings, and returned to the path of duty, which was rather 'a hard road to travel' just then. The house had been a hotel before hospitals were needed, and many of the doors still bore their old names; some not so inappropriate as might be imagined, for my ward was in truth a ballroom, if gunshot wounds could christen it. Forty beds were prepared, many already tenanted by tired men who fell down anywhere, and drowsed till the smell of food roused them. Round the great stove was gathered, the dreariest group I ever saw – ragged, gaunt and pale, mud to the knees, with bloody bandages untouched since put on days before; many bundled up in blankets, coats being lost or useless; and all wearing that disheartened look which proclaimed defeat, more plainly than any telegram of the Burnside blunder I pitied them so much, I dared not speak to them, though, remembering all they had been through since the route at Fredericksburg, I yearned to serve the dreariest of them all. Presently, Miss Blank tore me from my refuge behind piles of one-sleeved shirts, odd socks, bandages and lint; put basin, sponge, towels, and a block of brown soap into my hands, with these appalling directions: 'Come, my dear, begin to wash as fast as you can. Tell them to take off socks, coats and shirts, scrub them well, put on clean shirts, and the attendants will finish them off, and lay them in bed.'

If she had requested me to shave them all, or dance a hornpipe on the stove funnel, I should have been less staggered; but to scrub some dozen lords of creation at a moment's notice, was really – really. However, there was no time for nonsense, and, having resolved when I came to do everything I was bid, I drowned my scruples in my washbowl, clutched my soap manfully, and, assuming a business-like air, made a dab at the first dirty specimen I saw, bent on performing my task *vi et armis* if necessary. I chanced to light on a withered old Irishman, wounded in the head, which caused that portion of his frame to be tastefully laid out like a garden, the bandages being the walks, his hair the shrubbery. He was so overpowered by the honor of having a lady wash him, as he expressed it, that he did nothing but roll up his eyes, and bless me, in an irresistible style which was too much for my sense of the ludicrous; so we laughed together, and when I knelt down to take off his shoes, he 'flopped' also, and wouldn't hear of my touching 'them dirty craters. May your bed above be aisy darlin', for the day's work ye ar doon! Whoosh! there ye are, and bedad, it's hard tellin' which is the dirtiest, the fut or the shoe.'

It was; and if he hadn't been to the fore, I should have gone on pulling, under the impression that the 'fut' was a boot, for trousers, socks, shoes and legs were a mass of mud. This comical tableau produced a general grin, at which propitious beginning I took heart and scrubbed away like any tidy parent on a Saturday night. Some of them took the performance like sleepy children, leaning their tired heads against me as I worked, others looked grimly scandalized, and several of the roughest colored like bashful girls. One wore a soiled little bag about his neck, and, as I moved it, to bathe his wounded breast, I said: 'Your talisman didn't save you, did it?'

'Well, I reckon it did, marm, for that shot would a gone a couple a inches deeper but for my old mammy's camphor bag,' answered the cheerful philosopher.

Another, with a gunshot wound through the cheek, asked for a looking glass, and when I brought one, regarded his swollen face with a dolorous expression, as he muttered: 'I vow to gosh, that's too bad! I warn't a bad looking chap before, and now I'm done for; won't there be a thunderin' scar? And what on earth will Josephine Skinner say?'

He looked up at me with his one eye so appealingly, that I controlled my risibles, and assured him that if Josephine was a girl of sense, she would admire the honorable scar, as a lasting proof that he had faced the enemy, for all women thought a wound the best decoration a brave soldier could wear. I hope Miss Skinner verified the good opinion I so rashly expressed of her, but I shall never know.

The next scrubbee was a nice looking lad, with a curly brown mane, and a budding trace of gingerbread over the lip, which he called his beard, and defended stoutly, when the barber jocosely suggested its immolation. He lay on a bed, with one leg gone, and the right arm so shattered that it must evidently follow: yet the little Sergeant was as merry as if his afflictions were not worth lamenting over; and when a drop or two of salt water mingled with my suds at the sight of this strong young body, so marred and maimed, the boy looked up, with a brave smile, though there was a little quiver of the lips, as he said: 'Now don't you fret yourself about me, miss; I'm first rate here, for it's nuts to lie still on this bed, after knocking about in those confounded ambulances, that shake what there is left of a fellow to jelly. I never was in one of these places before, and think this cleaning up a jolly thing for us, though I'm afraid it isn't for you ladies.'

'Is this your first battle, Sergeant?'

'No, miss; I've been in six scrimmages, and never got a scratch till this last one; but it's done the business pretty thoroughly for me, I should say. Lord! What a scramble there'll be for arms and legs, when we old boys come out of our graves, on the Judgment Day: wonder if we shall get our own again? If we do, my leg will have to tramp from Fredericksburg, my arm from here, I suppose, and meet my body, wherever it may be.'

The fancy seemed to tickle him mightily, for he laughed blithely, and so did I; which, no doubt, caused the new nurse to be regarded as a light-minded sinner by the Chaplain, who roamed vaguely about, informing the men that they were all worms, corrupt of heart, with perishable bodies, and souls only to be saved by a diligent perusal of certain tracts, and other equally cheering bits of spiritual consolation, when spirituous ditto would have been preferred.

. . . Observing that the man next him had left his meal untouched, I offered the same service I had performed for his neighbor, but he shook his head.

'Thank you, ma'am; I don't think I'll ever eat again, for I'm shot in the stomach. But I'd like a drink of water, if you ain't too busy.'

I rushed away, but the water pails were gone to be refilled, and it was some time before they reappeared. I did not forget my patient, meanwhile, and, with the first mugful, hurried back to him. He seemed asleep; but something in the tired white face caused me to lis-

ten at his lips for a breath. None came. I touched his
forehead; it was cold: and then I knew that, while he
waited, a better nurse than I had given him a cooler
draught, and healed him with a touch. I laid the sheet
over the quiet sleeper, whom no noise could now dis-
turb; and, half an hour later, the bed was empty. It
seemed a poor requital for all he had sacrificed and
suffered on that hospital bed, lonely even in a crowd;
for there was no familiar face for him to look his last
upon; no friendly voice to say, 'Goodbye'; no hand to
lead him gently down into the Valley of the Shadow;
and he vanished, like a drop in that red sea upon
whose shores so many women stand lamenting. For a
moment I felt bitterly indignant at this seeming care-
lessness of the value of life, the sanctity of death; then
consoled myself with the thought that, when the great
muster roll was called, these nameless men might be
promoted above many whose tall monuments record
the barren honors they have won.

All having eaten, drank, and rested, the surgeons
began their rounds; and I took my first lesson in the
art of dressing wounds. It wasn't a festive scene, by any
means; for Dr P., whose aid I constituted myself, fell to
work with a vigor which soon convinced me that I was
a weaker vessel, though nothing would have induced
me to confess it then. He had served in the Crimea,
and seemed to regard a dilapidated body very much
as I should have regarded a damaged garment; and,
turning up his cuffs, whipped out a very unpleasant

looking housewife, cutting, sawing, patching and piecing, with the enthusiasm of an accomplished surgical seamstress; explaining the process, in scientific terms, to the patient, meantime; which, of course, was immensely cheering and comfortable. There was an uncanny sort of fascination in watching him, as he peered and probed into the mechanism of those wonderful bodies, whose mysteries he understood so well. The more intricate the wound, the better he liked it. A poor private, with both legs off, and shot through the lungs, possessed more attractions for him than a dozen generals, slightly scratched in some 'masterly retreat'; and had anyone appeared in small pieces, requesting to be put together again, he would have considered it a special dispensation.

The amputations were reserved till the morrow, and the merciful magic of ether was not thought necessary that day, so the poor souls had to bear their pains as best they might. It is all very well to talk of the patience of woman; and far be it from me to pluck that feather from her cap, for, heaven knows, she isn't allowed to wear many; but the patient endurance of these men, under trials of the flesh, was truly wonderful. Their fortitude seemed contagious, and scarcely a cry escaped them, though I often longed to groan for them, when pride kept their white lips shut, while great drops stood upon their foreheads, and the bed shook with the irrepressible tremor of their tortured bodies. One or two Irishmen anathematized the doctors with the frankness of their nation, and ordered the Virgin to stand by them, as if she had been the wedded Biddy to whom they could administer the poker, if she didn't; but, as a general thing, the work went on in silence, broken only by some quiet request for roller, instruments, or plaster, a sigh from the patient, or a sympathizing murmur from the nurse.

It was long past noon before these repairs were even partially made; and, having got the bodies of my boys into something like order, the next task was to minister to their minds, by writing letters to the anxious souls at home; answering questions, reading papers, taking possession of money and valuables; for the eighth commandment was reduced to a very fragmentary condition, both by the blacks and whites, who ornamented our hospital with their presence. Pocket books, purses, miniatures, and watches, were sealed up, labelled, and handed over to the matron, till such times as the owners thereof were ready to depart homeward or campward again. The letters dictated to me, and revised by me, that afternoon, would have made an excellent chapter for some future history of the war; for, like that which Thackeray's 'Ensign Spooney' wrote his mother just before Waterloo, they were 'full of affection, pluck, and bad spelling'; nearly all giving lively accounts of the battle, and ending with a somewhat sudden plunge from patriotism to provender, desiring 'Marm', 'Mary Ann', or 'Aunt Peters', to send along some pies, pickles, sweet stuff, and apples, 'to yourn in haste', Joe, Sam, or Ned, as the case might be.

My little Sergeant insisted on trying to scribble something with his left hand, and patiently accomplished some half dozen lines of hieroglyphics, which he gave me to fold and direct, with a boyish blush, that rendered a glimpse of 'My Dearest Jane', unnecessary, to assure me that the heroic lad had been more successful in the service of Commander-in-Chief Cupid than that of Gen. Mars; and a charming little romance blossomed instanter in Nurse Periwinkle's romantic fancy, though no further confidences were made that day, for Sergeant fell asleep, and, judging from his tranquil face, visited his absent sweetheart in the pleasant land of dreams.

At five o'clock a great bell rang, and the attendants flew, not to arms, but to their trays, to bring up supper, when a second uproar announced that it was ready. The newcomers woke at the sound; and I presently discovered that it took a very bad wound to incapacitate the defenders of the faith for the consumption of their rations; the amount that some of them sequestered was amazing; but when I suggested the probability of a famine hereafter, to the matron, that motherly lady cried out: 'Bless their hearts, why shouldn't they eat? It's their only amusement; so fill everyone, and, if there's not enough ready tonight, I'll lend my share to the Lord by giving it to the boys.' And, whipping up her coffee pot and plate of toast, she gladdened the eyes and stomachs of two or three dissatisfied heroes, by serving them with a liberal hand; and I haven't the slightest doubt that, having cast her bread upon the waters, it came back buttered, as another large-hearted old lady was wont to say.

Then came the doctor's evening visit; the administration of medicines; washing feverish faces; smoothing tumbled beds; wetting wounds; singing lullabies; and preparations for the night. By twelve, the last labor of love was done; the last 'good night' spoken; and, if any needed a reward for that day's work, they surely received it, in the silent eloquence of those long lines of faces, showing pale and peaceful in the shaded rooms, as we quitted them, followed by grateful glances that lighted us to bed, where rest, the sweetest, made our pillows soft, while Night and Nature took our places, filling that great house of pain with the healing miracles of Sleep, and his diviner brother, Death.

Chapter Four: A Night

Being fond of the night side of nature, I was soon promoted to the post of night nurse, with every facility for indulging in my favorite pastime of 'owling'. My colleague, a black-eyed widow, relieved me at dawn, we two taking care of the ward, between us, like the immortal Sairy and Betsey, 'turn and turn about'. I usually found my boys in the jolliest state of mind their condition allowed; for it was a known fact that Nurse

Periwinkle objected to blue devils, and entertained a belief that he who laughed most was surest of recovery. At the beginning of my reign, dumps and dismals prevailed; the nurses looked anxious and tired, the men gloomy or sad; and a general 'Hark! From-the-tombs-a-doleful-sound' style of conversation seemed to be the fashion: a state of things which caused one coming from a merry, social New England town, to feel as if she had got into an exhausted receiver; and the instinct of self-preservation, to say nothing of a philanthropic desire to serve the race, caused a speedy change in Ward No. 1.

More flattering than the most gracefully turned compliment, more grateful than the most admiring glance, was the sight of those rows of faces, all strange to me a little while ago, now lighting up, with smiles of welcome, as I came among them, enjoying that moment heartily, with a womanly pride in their regard, a motherly affection for them all. The evenings were spent in reading aloud, writing letters, waiting on and amusing the men, going the rounds with Dr P., as he made his second daily survey, dressing my dozen wounds afresh, giving last doses, and making them cozy for the long hours to come, till the nine o'clock bell rang, the gas was turned down, the day nurses went off duty, the night watch came on, and my nocturnal adventure began.

My ward was now divided into three rooms; and, under favor of the matron, I had managed to sort out the patients in such a way that I had what I called 'my duty room', my 'pleasure room', and my 'pathetic room', and worked for each in a different way. One, I visited, armed with a dressing tray, full of rollers, plasters, and pins; another, with books, flowers, games, and gossip; a third, with teapots, lullabies, consolation, and sometimes, a shroud.

Wherever the sickest or most helpless man chanced to be, there I held my watch, often visiting the other rooms, to see that the general watchman of the ward did his duty by the fires and the wounds, the latter needing constant wetting. Not only on this account did I meander, but also to get fresher air than the close rooms afforded; for, owing to the stupidity of that mysterious 'somebody' who does all the damage in the world, the windows had been carefully nailed down above, and the lower sashes could only be raised in the mildest weather, for the men lay just below. I had suggested a summary smashing of a few panes here and there, when frequent appeals to headquarters had proved unavailing, and daily orders to lazy attendants had come to nothing. No one seconded the motion, however, and the nails were far beyond my reach; for, though belonging to the sisterhood of 'ministering angels', I had no wings, and might as well have asked for Jacob's ladder, as a pair of steps, in that charitable chaos.

One of the harmless ghosts who bore me company during the haunted hours, was Dan, the watchman, whom I regarded with a certain awe; for, though so much together, I never fairly saw his face, and, but for his legs, should never have recognized him, as we seldom met by day. These legs were remarkable, as was his whole figure, for his body was short, rotund, and done up in a big jacket, and muffler; his beard hid the lower part of his face, his hat brim the upper; and all I ever discovered was a pair of sleepy eyes, and a very mild voice. But the legs! Very long, very thin, very crooked and feeble, looking like gray sausages in their tight coverings, without a ray of pegtopishness about them, and finished off with a pair of expansive, green cloth shoes, very like Chinese junks, with the sails down. This figure, gliding noiselessly about the dimly lighted rooms, was strongly suggestive of the spirit of a beer barrel mounted on corkscrews, haunting the old hotel in search of its lost mates, emptied and staved in long ago.

Another goblin who frequently appeared to me, was the attendant of the pathetic room, who, being a faithful soul, was often up to tend two or three men, weak and wandering as babies, after the fever had gone. The amiable creature beguiled the watches of the night by brewing jorums of a fearful beverage, which he called coffee, and insisted on sharing with me; coming in with a great bowl of something like mud soup, scalding hot, guiltless of cream, rich in an all-pervading flavor of molasses, scorch and tin pot. Such an amount of good will and neighborly kindness also went into the mess, that I never could find the heart to refuse, but always received it with thanks, sipped it with hypocritical relish while he remained, and whipped it into the slop jar the instant he departed, thereby gratifying him, securing one rousing laugh in the doziest hour of the night, and no one was the worse for the transaction but the pigs. Whether they were 'cut off untimely in their sins', or not, I carefully abstained from inquiring.

It was a strange life: asleep half the day, exploring Washington the other half, and all night hovering, like a massive cherubim, in a red rigolette, over the slumbering sons of man. I liked it, and found many things to amuse, instruct, and interest me. The snores alone were quite a study, varying from the mild sniff to the stentorian snort, which startled the echoes and hoisted the performer erect to accuse his neighbor of the deed, magnanimously forgive him, and wrapping the drapery of his couch about him, lie down to vocal slumber. After listening for a week to this band of wind instruments, I indulged in the belief that I could recognize each by the snore alone, and was tempted to join the chorus by breaking out with John Brown's favorite hymn: 'Blow Ye the Trumpet, Blow'!

I would have given much to have possessed the art of sketching, for many of the faces became wonderfully interesting when unconscious. Some grew stern and grim, the men evidently dreaming of war, as they gave orders, groaned over their wounds, or damned the rebels vigorously; some grew sad and infinitely pathetic, as if the pain borne silently all day, revenged itself by now betraying what the man's pride had concealed so well. Often the roughest grew young and pleasant when sleep smoothed the hard lines away, letting the real nature assert itself; many almost seemed to speak, and I learned to know these men better by night than through any intercourse by day. Sometimes they disappointed me, for faces that looked merry and good in the light, grew bad and sly when the shadows came . . .

A few talked busily; one drummer boy sang sweetly, though no persuasions could win a note from him by day; and several depended on being told what they had talked of in the morning. Even my constitutionals in the chilly halls, possessed a certain charm, for the house was never still. Sentinels tramped round it all night long, their muskets glittering in the wintry moonlight as they walked, or stood before the doors, straight and silent, as figures of stone, causing one to conjure up romantic visions of guarded forts, sudden surprises, and daring deeds; for in these war times the hum drum life of Yankeedom had vanished, and the most prosaic feel some thrill of that excitement which stirs the nation's heart, and makes its capital a camp of hospitals. Wandering up and down these lower halls, I often heard cries from above, steps hurrying to and fro, saw surgeons passing up, or men coming down carrying a stretcher, where lay a long white figure, whose face was shrouded and whose fight was done. Sometimes I stopped to watch the passers in the street, the moonlight shining on the spire opposite, or the gleam of some vessel floating, like a white-winged seagull, down the broad Potomac, whose fullest flow can never wash away the red stain of the land.

The night whose events I have a fancy to record, opened with a little comedy, and closed with a great tragedy; for a virtuous and useful life untimely ended is always tragical to those who see not as God sees. My headquarters were beside the bed of a New Jersey boy, crazed by the horrors of that dreadful Saturday. A slight wound in the knee brought him there; but his mind had suffered more than his body; some string of that delicate machine was over strained, and, for days, he had been reliving in imagination, the scenes he could not forget, till his distress broke out in incoherent ravings, pitiful to hear As I sat by him, endeavoring to soothe his poor distracted brain by the constant touch of wet hands over his hot forehead, he lay cheering his comrades on, hurrying them back, then counting them as they fell around him, often clutching my arm, to drag me from the vicinity of a bursting shell, or covering up his head to screen himself from a shower of shot; his face brilliant with fever; his eyes restless; his head never still; every muscle strained and rigid; while an incessant stream of defiant shouts, whispered warnings, and broken laments, poured from his lips with that forceful bewilderment which makes such wanderings so hard to overhear.

It was past eleven, and my patient was slowly wearying himself into fitful intervals of quietude, when, in one of these pauses, a curious sound arrested my attention. Looking over my shoulder, I saw a one-legged phantom hopping nimbly down the room; and, going to meet it, recognized a certain Pennsylvania gentleman, whose wound fever had taken a turn for the worse, and, depriving him of the few wits a drunken campaign had left him, set him literally tripping on the light, fantastic toe 'toward home', as he blandly informed me, touching the military cap which formed a striking contrast to the severe simplicity of the rest of his decidedly undress uniform. When sane, the least movement produced a roar of pain or a volley of oaths; but the departure of reason seemed to have wrought an agreeable change, both in the man and his manners; for, balancing himself on one leg, like a meditative stork, he plunged into an animated discussion of the war, the President, lager beer, and Enfield rifles, regardless of any suggestions of mine as to the propriety of returning to bed, lest he be court-martialed for desertion.

Anything more supremely ridiculous can hardly be imagined than this figure, scantily draped in white, its one foot covered with a big blue sock, a dingy cap set rakingly askew on its shaven head, and placid satisfaction beaming in its broad red face, as it flourished a mug in one hand, an old boot in the other, calling them canteen and knapsack, while it skipped and fluttered in the most unearthly fashion. What to do with the creature I didn't know; Dan was absent, and if I went to find him, the perambulator might festoon himself out of the window, set his toga on fire, or do some of his neighbors a mischief. The attendant of the room was sleeping like a near relative of the celebrated Seven, and nothing short of pins would rouse him; for he had been out that day, and whiskey asserted its supremacy in balmy whiffs. Still declaiming, in a fine flow of eloquence, the demented gentleman hopped on, blind and deaf to my graspings and entreaties; and I was about to slam the door in his face, and run for help, when a second and saner phantom, 'all in white', came to the rescue, in the likeness of a big Prussian, who spoke no English, but divined the crisis, and put an end to it, by bundling the lively monoped into his bed, like a baby, with an authoritative command to 'stay put', which received added weight from being delivered in an odd conglomeration of French and German, accompanied by warning wags of a head decorated with a yellow cotton nightcap, rendered most imposing by a tassel like a bell-pull.

Rather exhausted by his excursion, the member from Pennsylvania subsided; and, after an irrepressible laugh together, my Prussian ally and myself were returning to our places, when the echo of a sob caused us to glance along the beds. It came from one in the corner – such a little bed! – and such a tearful little face looked up at us, as we stopped beside it! The twelve-year-old drummer boy was not singing now, but sobbing, with a manly effort all the while to stifle the distressful sounds that would break out.

'What is it, Teddy?' I asked, as he rubbed the tears away, and checked himself in the middle of a great sob to answer plaintively.

'I've got a chill, ma'am, but I ain't cryin' for that, 'cause I'm used to it. I dreamed Kit was here, and when I waked up he wasn't, and I couldn't help it, then.'

The boy came in with the rest, and the man who was taken dead from the ambulance was the Kit he mourned. Well he might; for, when the wounded were brought from Fredericksburg, the child lay in one of the camps thereabout, and this good friend, though sorely hurt himself, would not leave him to the exposure and neglect of such a time and place; but, wrapping him in his own blanket, carried him in his arms to the transport, tended him during the passage, and only yielded up his charge when Death met him at the door of the hospital which promised care and comfort for the boy. For ten days, Teddy had shivered or burned with fever and ague, pining the while for Kit, and refusing to be comforted, because he had not been able to thank him for the generous protection, which, perhaps, had cost the giver's life. The vivid dream had wrung the childish heart with a fresh pang, and when I tried the solace fitted for his years, the remorseful fear that haunted him found vent in a fresh burst of tears, as he looked at the wasted hands I was endeavoring to warm: 'Oh! if I'd only been as thin when Kit carried me as I am now, maybe he wouldn't have died; but I was heavy, he was hurt worser than we knew, and so it killed him; and I didn't see him, to say goodbye.'

This thought had troubled him in secret; and my assurances that his friend would probably have died at all events, hardly assuaged the bitterness of his regretful grief.

At this juncture, the delirious man began to shout; the one-legged rose up in his bed, as if preparing for another dart, Teddy bewailed himself more piteously than before: and if ever a woman was at her wit's end, that distracted female was Nurse Periwinkle, during the space of two or three minutes, as she vibrated between the three beds, like an agitated pendulum. Like a most opportune reinforcement, Dan, the bandy, appeared, and devoted himself to the lively party, leaving me free to return to my post; for the Prussian, with a nod and a smile, took the lad away to his own bed, and lulled him to sleep with a soothing murmur, like a mammoth humble bee. I liked that in Fritz, and if he ever wondered afterward at the dainties which sometimes found their way into his rations, or the extra comforts of his bed, he might have found a solution of the mystery in sundry persons' knowledge of the fatherly action of that night.

Hardly was I settled again, when the inevitable bowl appeared, and its bearer delivered a message I had expected, yet dreaded to receive.

'John is going, ma'am, and wants to see you, if you can come.'

'The moment this boy is asleep; tell him so, and let me know if I am in danger of being too late.'

My Ganymede departed, and while I quieted poor Shaw, I thought of John. He came in a day or two after the others; and, one evening, when I entered my 'pathetic room', I found a lately emptied bed occupied by a large, fair man, with a fine face, and the serenest eyes I ever met. One of the earlier comers had often spoken of a friend, who had remained behind, that those apparently worse wounded than himself might reach a shelter first. It seemed a David and Jonathan sort of friendship. The man fretted for his mate, and was never tired of praising John – his courage, sobriety, self-denial, and unfailing kindliness of heart; always winding up with:

'He's an out an' out fine feller, ma'am; you see if he ain't.'

I had some curiosity to behold this piece of excellence, and when he came, watched him for a night or two, before I made friends with him; for, to tell the truth, I was a little afraid of the stately looking man, whose bed had to be lengthened to accommodate his commanding stature; who seldom spoke, uttered no complaint, asked no sympathy, but tranquilly observed what went on about him; and, as he lay high upon his pillows, no picture of dying stateman or warrior was ever fuller of real dignity than this Virginia blacksmith. A most attractive face he had, framed in brown hair and beard, comely featured and full of vigor, as yet unsubdued by pain; thoughtful and often beautifully mild while watching the afflictions of others, as if entirely forgetful of his own. His mouth was grave and firm, with plenty of will and courage in its lines, but a smile could make it as sweet as any woman's; and his eyes were child's eyes, looking one fairly in the face, with a clear, straightforward glance, which promised well for such as placed their faith in him. He seemed to cling to life, as if it were rich in duties and delights, and he had learned the secret of content. The only time I saw his composure disturbed, was when my surgeon brought another to examine John, who scrutinized their faces with an anxious look, asking of the elder: 'Do you think I shall pull through, sir?'

'I hope so, my man.'

And, as the two passed on, John's eye still followed them, with an intentness which would have won a clearer answer from them, had they seen it. A momentary shadow flitted over his face; then came the usual serenity, as if, in that brief eclipse, he had acknowledged the existence of some hard possibility, and, asking nothing yet hoping all things, left the issue in God's hands, with that submission which is true piety.

The next night, as I went my rounds with Dr P., I happened to ask which man in the room probably suffered most; and, to my great surprise, he glanced at John.

'Every breath he draws is like a stab; for the ball pierced the left lung, broke a rib, and did no end of damage here and there; so the poor lad can find neither forgetfulness nor ease, because he must lie on his wounded back or suffocate. It will be a hard struggle, and a long one, for he possesses great vitality; but even his temperate life can't save him; I wish it could.'

'You don't mean he must die, Doctor?'

'Bless you there's not the slightest hope for him; and you'd better tell him so before long; women have a way of doing such things comfortably, so I leave it to you. He won't last more than a day or two, at furthest.'

I could have sat down on the spot and cried heartily, if I had not learned the wisdom of bottling up one's tears for leisure moments. Such an end seemed very hard for such a man, when half a dozen worn out, worthless bodies round him, were gathering up the remnants of wasted lives, to linger on for years perhaps, burdens to others, daily reproaches to themselves. The army needed men like John, earnest, brave, and faithful fighting for liberty and justice with both heart and hand, true soldiers of the Lord. I could not give him up so soon, or think with any patience of so excellent a nature robbed of its fulfillment, and blundered into eternity by the rashness or stupidity of those at whose hands so many lives may be required. It was an easy thing for Dr P. to say: 'Tell him he must die,' but a cruelly hard thing to do, and by no means as 'comfortable' as he politely suggested. I had not the heart to do it then, and privately indulged the hope that some change for the better might take place, in spite of gloomy prophesies; so, rendering my task unnecessary.

A few minutes later, as I came in again, with fresh rollers, I saw John sitting erect, with no one to support him, while the surgeon dressed his back. I had never hitherto seen it done; for, having simpler wounds to attend to, and knowing the fidelity of the attendant, I had left John to him, thinking it might be more agreeable and safe; for both strength and experience were needed in his case. I had forgotten that the strong man might long for the gentle tendance of a woman's hands, the sympathetic magnetism of a woman's presence, as well as the feebler souls about him.

The Doctor's words caused me to reproach myself with neglect, not of any real duty perhaps, but of those little cares and kindnesses that solace homesick spirits, and make the heavy hours pass easier. John looked lonely and forsaken just then, as he sat with bent head, hands folded on his knee, and no outward sign of suffering, till, looking nearer, I saw great tears roll down and drop upon the floor. It was a new sight there; for, though I had seen many suffer, some swore, some groaned, most endured silently, but none wept. Yet it did not seem weak, only very touching, and straightway my fear vanished, my heart opened wide and took him in, as, gathering the bent head in my arms, as freely as if he had been a little child, I said: 'Let me help you bear it, John.'

Never, on any human countenance, have I seen so swift and beautiful a look of gratitude, surprise and comfort, as that which answered me more eloquently than the whispered: 'Thank you, ma'am, this is right good! this is what I wanted!'

'Then why not ask for it before?'

'I didn't like to be a trouble; you seemed so busy, and I could manage to get on alone.'

'You shall not want it anymore, John.'

Nor did he; for now I understood the wistful look that sometimes followed me, as I went out, after a brief pause beside his bed, or merely a passing nod, while busied with those who seemed to need me more than he, because more urgent in their demands; now I knew that to him, as to so many, I was the poor substitute for mother, wife, or sister, and in his eyes no stranger, but a friend who hitherto had seemed neglectful; for, in his modesty, he had never guessed the truth. This was changed now; and, through the tedious operation of probing, bathing, and dressing his wounds, he leaned against me, holding my hand fast, and, if pain wrung further tears from him, no one saw them fall but me. When he was laid down again, I hovered about him, in a remorseful state of mind that would not let me rest, till I had bathed his face, brushed his 'bonny brown hair', set all things smooth about him, and laid a knot of heath and heliotrope on his clean pillow.

While doing this, he watched me with the satisfied expression I so liked to see; and when I offered the little nosegay, held it carefully in his great hand, smoothed a ruffled leaf or two, surveyed and smelt it with an air of genuine delight, and lay contentedly regarding the glimmer of the sunshine on the green. Although the manliest man among my forty, he said: 'Yes, ma'am,' like a little boy; received suggestions for his comfort with the quick smile that brightened his whole face; and now and then, as I stood tidying the table by his bed, I felt him softly touch my gown, as if to assure himself that I was there. Anything more natural and frank I never saw, and found this brave John as bashful as brave, yet full of excellencies and fine aspirations, which, having no power to express themselves in words, seemed to have bloomed into his character and made him what he was.

After that night, an hour of each evening that remained to him was devoted to his ease or pleasure. He could not talk much, for breath was precious, and he spoke in whispers; but from occasional conversations, I gleaned scraps of private history which only added to the affection and respect I felt for him. Once he asked me to write a letter, and as I settled pen and paper, I said, with an irrepressible glimmer of feminine curiosity: 'Shall it be addressed to Wife, or Mother, John?'

'Neither, ma'am; I've got no wife, and will write to Mother myself when I get better. Did you think I was married because of this?' he asked, touching a plain ring he wore, and often turned thoughtfully on his finger when he lay alone.

'Partly that, but more from a settled sort of look you have; a look which young men seldom get until they marry.'

'I didn't know that; but I'm not so very young, ma'am, thirty in May, and have been what you might call settled this ten years; for Mother's a widow, I'm the oldest child she has, and it wouldn't do for me to marry until Lizzy has a home of her own, and Laurie's learned his trade; for we're not rich, and I must be father to the children and husband to the dear old woman, if I can.'

'No doubt but you are both, John; yet how came you to go to war, if you felt so? Wasn't enlisting as bad as marrying?'

'No, ma'am, not as I see it, for one is helping my neighbor, the other pleasing myself. I went because I couldn't help it. I didn't want the glory or the pay; I wanted the right thing done, and people kept saying the men who were in earnest ought to fight. I was in earnest, the Lord knows! but I held off as long as I could, not knowing which was my duty; Mother saw the case, gave me her ring to keep me steady, and said: "Go", so I went.'

A short story and a simple one, but the man and the mother were portrayed better than pages of fine writing could have done it.

'Do you ever regret that you came, when you lie here suffering so much?'

'Never, ma'am; I haven't helped a great deal, but

I've shown I was willing to give my life, and perhaps I've got to; but I don't blame anybody, and if it was to do over again, I'd do it. I'm a little sorry I wasn't wounded in front; it looks cowardly to be hit in the back, but I obeyed orders, and it don't matter in the end, I know.'

Poor John! It did not matter now, except that a shot in the front might have spared the long agony in store for him. He seemed to read the thought that troubled me, as he spoke so hopefully when there was no hope, for he suddenly added: 'This is my first battle; do they think it's going to be my last?'

'I'm afraid they do, John.'

It was the hardest question I had ever been called upon to answer; doubly hard with those clear eyes fixed on mine, forcing a truthful answer by their own truth. He seemed a little startled at first, pondered over the fateful fact a moment, then shook his head, with a glance at the broad chest and muscular limbs stretched out before him: 'I'm not afraid, but it's difficult to believe all at once. I'm so strong it don't seem possible for such a little wound to kill me.'

''Tis not so deep as a well, nor so wide as a church door, but 'tis enough.'

And John would have said the same could he have seen the ominous black holes between his shoulders; he never had; and, seeing the ghastly lights about him, could not believe his own wound more fatal than these, for all the suffering it caused him.

'Shall I write to your mother, now?' I asked, thinking that these sudden tidings might change all plans and purposes; but they did not; for the man received the order of the Divine Commander to march with the same unquestioning obedience with which the soldier had received that of the human one; doubtless remembering that the first led him to life, and the last to death.

'No, ma'am; to Laurie just the same; he'll break it to her best, and I'll add a line to her myself when you get done.'

So I wrote the letter which he dictated, finding it better than any I had sent; for, though here and there a little ungrammatical or inelegant, each sentence came to me briefly worded, but most expressive; full of excellent counsel to the boy, tenderly bequeathing 'Mother and Lizzie' to his care, and bidding him goodbye in words the sadder for their simplicity. He added a few lines, with steady hand, and, as I sealed it, said, with a patient sort of sigh: 'I hope the answer will come in time for me to see it'; then, turning away his face, laid the flowers against his lips, as if to hide some quiver of emotion at the thought of such a sudden sundering of all the dear home ties.

These things had happened two days before; now John was dying, and the letter had not come. I had been summoned to many death beds in my life, but to none that made my heart ache as it did then, since my mother called me to watch the departure of a spirit akin to this in its gentleness and patient strength. As I went in, John stretched out both hands: 'I knew you'd come! I guess I'm moving on, ma'am.'

He was; and so rapidly that, even while he spoke, over his face I saw the gray veil falling that no human hand can lift. I sat down by him, wiped the drops from his forehead, stirred the air about him with the slow wave of a fan, and waited to help him die. He stood in sore need of help – and I could do so little; for, as the doctor had foretold, the strong body rebelled against death, and fought every inch of the way, forcing him to draw each breath with a spasm, and clench his hands with an imploring look, as if he asked: 'How long must I endure this, and be still!'

For hours he suffered dumbly, without a moment's respire, or a moment's murmuring; his limbs grew cold, his face damp, his lips white, and, again and again, he tore the covering off his breast, as if the lightest weight added to his agony; yet through it all, his eyes never lost their perfect serenity, and the man's soul seemed to sit therein, undaunted by the ills that vexed his flesh.

One by one, the men woke, and round the room appeared a circle of pale faces and watchful eyes, full of awe and pity; for, though a stranger, John was beloved by all. Each man there had wondered at his patience, respected his piety, admired his fortitude, and now lamented his hard death; for the influence of an upright nature had made itself deeply felt, even in one little week. Presently, the Jonathan who so loved this comely David, came creeping from his bed for a last look and word. The kind soul was full of trouble, as the choke in his voice, the grasp of his hand, betrayed; but there were no tears, and the farewell of the friends was the more touching for its brevity.

'Old boy, how are you?' faltered the one.

'Most through, thank heaven!' whispered the other.

'Can I say or do anything for you anywheres?'

'Take my things home, and tell them that I did my best.'

'I will! I will!'

'Goodbye, Ned.'

'Goodbye, John, goodbye!'

They kissed each other, tenderly as women, and so parted, for poor Ned could not stay to see his comrade die. For a little while, there was no sound in the room but the drip of water, from a stump or two, and John's distressful gasps, as he slowly breathed his life away. I thought him nearly gone, and had just laid down the fan, believing its help to be no longer needed, when suddenly he rose up in his bed, and cried out with a bitter cry that broke the silence, sharply startling everyone with its agonized appeal: 'For God's sake, give me air!'

It was the only cry pain or death had wrung from him, the only boon he had asked; and none of us could grant it, for all the airs that blew were useless now. Dan flung up the window. The first red streak of dawn was warming the gray east, a herald of the coming sun; John saw it, and with the love of light which lingers in us to the end, seemed to read in it a sign of hope of help, for, over his whole face there broke that mysterious expression, brighter than any smile, which often comes to eyes that look their last. He laid himself gently down; and, stretching out his strong right arm, as if to grasp and bring the blessed air to his lips in a fuller flow, lapsed into a merciful unconsciousness, which assured us that for him suffering was forever past. He died then; for, though the heavy breaths still tore their way up for a little longer, they were but the waves of an ebbing tide that beat unfelt against the wreck, which an immortal voyager had deserted with a smile. He never spoke again, but to the end held my hand close, so close that when he was asleep at last, I could not draw it away. Dan helped me, warning me as he did so that it was unsafe for dead and living flesh to lie so long together; but though my hand was strangely cold and stiff, and four white marks remained across its back, even when warmth and color had returned elsewhere, I could not but be glad that, through its touch, the presence of human sympathy, perhaps, had lightened that hard hour.

When they had made him ready for the grave, John lay in state for half an hour, a thing which seldom happened in that busy place; but a universal sentiment of reverence and affection seemed to fill the hearts of all who had known or heard of him; and when the rumor of his death went through the house, always astir, many came to see him, and I felt a tender sort of pride in my lost patient; for he looked a most heroic figure, lying there stately and still as the statue of some young knight asleep upon his tomb. The lovely expression which so often beautifies dead faces, soon replaced the marks of pain, and I longed for those who loved him best to see him when half an hour's acquaintance with Death had made them friends. As we stood looking at him, the ward master handed me a letter, saying it had been forgotten the night before. It was John's letter, come just an hour too late to gladden the eyes that had longed and looked for it so eagerly yet he had it; for, after I had cut some brown locks for his mother, and taken off the ring to send her, telling how well the talisman had done its work, I kissed this good son for her sake, and laid the letter in his hand, still folded as when I drew my own away, feeling that its place was there, and making myself happy with the thought, that, even in his solitary place in the 'Government Lot', he would not be without some token of the love which makes life beautiful and outlives death. Then I left him, glad to have known so genuine a man, and carrying with me an enduring memory of the brave Virginia blacksmith, as he lay serenely waiting for the dawn of that long day which knows no night.

Chapter Five: Off Duty

'My dear girl, we shall have you sick in your bed, unless you keep yourself warm and quiet for a few days. Widow Wadman can take care of the ward alone, now the men are so comfortable, and have her vacation when you are about again. Now do be prudent in time, and don't let me have to add a Periwinkle to my bouquet of patients.'

This advice was delivered, in a paternal manner, by the youngest surgeon in the hospital, a kind-hearted little gentleman, who seemed to consider me a frail young blossom, that needed much cherishing, instead of a tough old spinster, who had been knocking about the world for thirty years. At the time I write of, he discovered me sitting on the stairs, with a nice cloud of unwholesome steam rising from the washroom; a party of January breezes disporting themselves in the halls; and perfumes, by no means from 'Araby the blest', keeping them company; while I enjoyed a fit of coughing, which caused my head to spin in a way that made the application of a cool banister both necessary and agreeable, as I waited for the frolicsome wind to restore the breath I'd lost; cheering myself, meantime, with a secret conviction that pneumonia was waiting for me round the corner. This piece of advice had been offered by several persons for a week, and refused by me with the obstinacy with which my sex is so richly gifted. But the last few hours had developed several surprising internal and external phenomena, which impressed upon me the fact that if I didn't make a masterly retreat very soon, I should tumble down somewhere, and have to be borne ignominiously from the field. My head felt like a cannon ball; my feet had a tendency to cleave to the floor; the walls at times undulated in a most disagreeable manner; people looked unnaturally big; and the 'very bottles on the mankle shelf' appeared to dance derisively before my eyes. Taking these things into consideration while blinking stupidly at Dr Z., I resolved to retire gracefully, if I must; so, with a valedictory to my boys, a private lecture to Mrs Wadman, and a fervent wish that I could take off my body and work in my soul, I mournfully ascended to my apartment, and Nurse P. was reported off duty.

For the benefit of any ardent damsel whose patriotic fancy may have surrounded hospital life with a halo of charms, I will briefly describe the bower to which I retired, in a somewhat ruinous condition. It was well ventilated, for five panes of glass had suffered compound fractures, which all the surgeons and nurses had failed to heal; the two windows were draped with sheets, the church hospital opposite being a brick-and-mortar Argus, and the female mind cherishing a prejudice in favor of retiracy during the night-capped periods of existence. A bare floor supported two narrow iron beds, spread with thin mattresses like plasters, furnished with pillows in the last stages of consumption. In a fireplace, guiltless of shovel, tongs, andirons, or grate, burned a log inch by inch, being too long to go on all at once; so, while the fire blazed away at one end, I did the same at the other, as I tripped over it a dozen times a day, and flew up to poke it a dozen times at night. A mirror (let us be elegant!) of the dimensions of a muffin, and about as reflective, hung over a tin basin, blue pitcher, and a brace of yellow mugs. Two invalid tables, ditto chairs, wandered here and there, and the closet contained a varied collection of bonnets, bottles, bags, boots, bread and butter, boxes and bugs. The closet was a regular Blue Beard cupboard to me; I always opened it with fear and trembling, owing to rats, and shut it in anguish of spirit; for time and space were not to be had, and chaos reigned along with the rats. Our chimney piece was decorated with a flat-iron, a Bible, a candle minus stick, a lavender bottle, a new tin pan, so brilliant that it served nicely for a pier glass, and such of the portly black bugs as preferred a warmer climate than the rubbish hole afforded. Two arks, commonly called trunks, lurked behind the door, containing the worldly goods of the twain who laughed and cried, slept and scrambled, in this refuge; while from the white-washed walls above either bed, looked down the pictured faces of those whose memory can make for us –

'One little room an everywhere.' . . .

Now, while I'm freeing my mind, I should like to enter my protest against employing convalescents as attendants, instead of strong, properly trained, and cheerful men. How it may be in other places I cannot say; but here it was a source of constant trouble and confusion, these feeble, ignorant men trying to sweep, scrub, lift, and wait upon their sicker comrades. One, with a diseased heart, was expected to run up and down stairs, carry heavy trays, and move helpless men; he tried it, and grew rapidly worse than when he first came: and, when he was ordered out to march away to the convalescent hospital, fell, in a sort of fit, before he turned the corner, and was brought back to die. Another, hurt by a fall from his horse, endeavored to do his duty, but failed entirely, and the wrath of the ward master fell upon the nurse, who must either scrub the rooms herself, or take the lecture; for the boy looked stout and well, and the master never happened to see him turn white with pain, or hear him groan in his sleep when an involuntary motion strained his poor back. Constant complaints were being made of incompetent attendants, and some dozen women did double duty, and then were blamed for breaking down. If any hospital director fancies this a good and economical arrangement, allow one used-up nurse to tell him it isn't, and beg him to spare the sisterhood, who sometimes, in their sympathy, forget that they are mortal, and run the risk of being made immortal, sooner than is agreeable to their partial friends.

. . . Shut up in my room, with no voice, spirits, or books, that week was not a holiday, by any means.

Finding meals a humbug, I stopped away altogether, trusting that if this sparrow was of any worth, the Lord would not let it fall to the ground. Like a flock of friendly ravens, my sister nurses fed me, not only with food for the body, but kind words for the mind; and soon, from being half starved, I found myself so be-teaed and be-toasted, petted and served, that I was quite 'in the lap of luxury', in spite of cough, headache, a painful consciousness of my pleura, and a realizing sense of bones in the human frame. From the pleasant house on the hill, the home in the heart of Washington, and the Willard caravansary, came friends new and old, with bottles, baskets, carriages and invitations for the invalid; and daily our Florence Nightingale climbed the steep stairs, stealing a moment from her busy life, to watch over the stranger, of whom she was as thoughtfully tender as any mother. Long may she wave! Whatever others may think or say, Nurse Periwinkle is forever grateful; and among her relics of that Washington defeat, none is more valued than the little book which appeared on her pillow, one dreary day; for the D. D. [Dorothea Dix] written in it means to her far more than Doctor of Divinity.

Being forbidden to meddle with fleshly arms and legs, I solaced myself by mending cotton ones, and, as I sat sewing at my window, watched the moving panorama that passed below; amusing myself with taking notes of the most striking figures in it. Long trains of army wagons kept up a perpetual rumble from morning till night; ambulances rattled to and fro with busy surgeons, nurses taking an airing, or convalescents going in parties to be fitted to artificial limbs. Strings of sorry looking horses passed, saying as plainly as dumb creatures could: 'Why, in a city full of them, is there no horse-pital for us?'

Often a cart came by, with several rough coffins in it and no mourners following; barouches, with invalid officers, rolled round the corner, and carriage loads of pretty children, with black coachmen, footmen, and maids. The women who took their walks abroad, were so extinguished in three-story bonnets, with over-hanging balconies of flowers, that their charms were obscured; and all I can say of them is that they dressed in the worst possible taste, and walked like ducks.

The men did the picturesque, and did it so well that Washington looked like a mammoth masquerade. Spanish hats, scarlet-lined riding cloaks, swords and sashes, high boots and bright spurs, beards and mustaches, which made plain faces comely, and comely faces heroic; these vanities of the flesh transformed our butchers, bakers, and candlestick makers into gallant riders of gaily caparisoned horses, much handsomer than themselves; and dozens of such figures were constantly prancing by, with private prickings of spurs, for the benefit of the perambulating flower bed. Some of these gentlemen affected painfully tight uniforms, and little caps, kept on by some new law of gravitation, as they covered only the bridge of the nose, yet never fell off; the men looked like stuffed fowls, and rode as if the safety of the nation depended on their speed alone. The fattest, grayest officers dressed most, and ambled statelily along, with orderlies behind, trying to look as if they didn't know the stout party in front, and doing much caracoling on their own account . . .

. . . I expected to have to defend myself from accusations of prejudice against color; but was surprised to find things just the other way, and daily shocked some neighbor by treating the blacks as I did the whites. The men would swear at the 'darkies', would put two gs into negro, and scoff at the idea of any good coming from such trash. The nurses were willing to be served by the colored people, but seldom thanked them, never praised, and scarcely recognized them in the street; whereat the blood of two generations of abolitionists waxed hot in my veins, and, at the first opportunity, proclaimed itself, and asserted the right of free speech as doggedly as the irrepressible Folsom herself.

Happening to catch up a funny little black baby, who was toddling about the nurses' kitchen, one day, when I went down to make a mess for some of my men, a Virginia woman standing by elevated her most prominent features, with a sniff of disapprobation, exclaiming: 'Gracious, Miss P.! How can you? I've been here six months, and never so much as touched the little toad with a poker.'

'More shame for you, ma'am,' responded Miss P.; and, with the natural perversity of a Yankee, followed up the blow by kissing 'the toad', with ardor. His face was providentially as clean and shiny as if his mamma had just polished it up with a corner of her apron and a drop from the tea-kettle spout, like old Aunt Chloe, This rash act, and the anti-slavery lecture that followed, while one hand stirred gruel for sick America, and the other hugged baby Africa, did not produce the cheering result which I fondly expected; for my comrade henceforth regarded me as a dangerous fanatic, and my protegé nearly came to his death by insisting on swarming upstairs to my room, on all occasions, and being walked on like a little black spider.

I waited for New Year's day with more eagerness than I had ever known before; and, though it brought me no gift, I felt rich in the act of justice so tardily performed toward some of those about me. As the bells rung midnight, I electrified my roommate by dancing out of bed, throwing up the window, and flapping my handkerchief, with a feeble cheer, in answer to the shout of a group of colored men in the street below. All night they tooted and tramped, fired crackers, sung 'Glory, Hallelujah', and took comfort, poor souls! In their own way. The sky was clear, the moon shone benignly, a mild wind blew across the river, and all good omens seemed to usher in the dawn of the day whose noontide cannot now be long in coming. If the colored people had taken hands and danced around the White House, with a few cheers for the much-abused gentleman who has immortalized himself by one just act, no president could have had a finer levee, or one to be prouder of.

While these lights and sounds were going on without, curious scenes were passing within, and I was learning that one of the best methods of fitting oneself to be a nurse in a hospital, is to be a patient there; for then only can one wholly realize what the men suffer and sigh for; how acts of kindness touch and win; how much or little we are to those about us; and for the first time really see that in coming there we have taken our lives in our hands, and may have to pay dearly for a brief experience. Everyone was very kind; the attendants of my ward often came up to report progress, to fill my wood box, or bring messages and presents from my boys. The nurses took many steps with those tired feet of theirs, and several came each evening, to chat over my fire and make things cozy for the night. The doctors paid daily visits, tapped at my lungs to see if pneumonia was within, left doses without names, and went away, leaving me as ignorant, and much more uncomfortable than when they came. Hours began to get confused; people looked odd; queer faces haunted the room, and the nights were one long fight with weariness and pain.

Letters from home grew anxious; the doctors lifted their eyebrows, and nodded ominously; friends said: 'Don't stay' and an internal rebellion seconded the advice; but the three months were not out, and the idea of giving up so soon was proclaiming a defeat before I was fairly routed; so to all 'Don't stays' I opposed 'I wills', till, one fine morning, a gray-headed gentleman rose like a welcome ghost on my hearth; and, at the sight of him, my resolution melted away, my heart turned traitor to my boys, and, when he said: 'Come home,' I answered: 'Yes, Father;' and so ended my career as an army nurse.

I never shall regret the going, though a sharp tussle with typhoid, ten dollars, and a wig, are all the visible results of the experiment; for one may live and learn much in a month. A good fit of illness proves the value of health; real danger tries one's mettle; and self-sacrifice sweetens character. Let no one who sincerely desires to help the work on in this way, delay going through any fear; for the worth of life lies in the experiences that fill it, and this is one which cannot be forgotten. All that is best and bravest in the hearts of men and women, comes out in scenes like these; and, though a hospital is a rough school, its lessons are both stern and salutary; and the humblest of pupils there, in proportion to his faithfulness, learns a deeper faith in God and in himself. I, for one, would return tomorrow, on the 'up-again-and-take-another' principle, if I could; for the amount of pleasure and profit I got out of that month compensates for all after pangs; and, though a sadly womanish feeling, I take some satisfaction in the thought that, if I could not lay my head on the altar of my country, I have my hair; and that is more than handsome Helen did for her dead husband, when she sacrificed only the ends of her ringlets on his urn. Therefore, I close this little chapter of hospital experiences, with the regret that they were no better worth recording; and add the poetical gem with which I console myself for the untimely demise of 'Nurse Periwinkle':

> Oh, lay her in a little pit,
> With a marble stone to cover it;
> And carve thereon a gruel spoon,
> To show a 'nuss' has died too soon.

Other titles from Notting Hill Editions*

Essays on the Self by Virginia Woolf
Introduced by Joanna Kavenna

Written between 1919, when Woolf was thirty-seven, and 1940, when she was fifty-eight, this extraordinary selection of essays includes discussions about the rights of women, the revolutions of modernity, the past, present and future of the novel and the inequalities and agonies of war, covering a period in Woolf's life when her opinions and her circumstances changed.

Drawn from Life: Selected Essays of Michel de Montaigne
Translated by M.A. Screech and Introduced by Tim Parks

In 1571, shortly after a near-death experience, Montaigne retired to a room in his tower where he began to write his famous essays. These 'whimsies' are intimate, revelatory and explore themes of fear and courage, mortality and personal freedom, ideas considered so dangerous that his books were banned by the Vatican for nearly two centuries. In his introduction, Tim Parks sheds new light on this enduringly popular figure.

The Russian Soul: Selections from A Writer's Diary
by Fyodor Dostoevsky
Introduced by Rosamund Bartlett

Dostoevsky's immediate impulse for embarking on *A Writer's Diary* in 1873 was a desire to come into closer contact with his readers. Far more popular than his novels ever were, it was a unique journalistic enterprise incorporating art and politics, intimate confession, criticism and short stories. Brilliantly introduced by distinguished scholar and writer Rosamund Bartlett, the *Diary* stands revealed as the work of a writer-activist who sought to transform Russian society.

*All titles are available in the UK, and some titles are available in the rest of the world. For more information please visit www.nottinghilleditions.com

A selection of our titles is distributed in the US and Canada by New York Review Books. For more information on available titles please visit www.nyrb.com